Glory Through Pain

An Athlete's True Story of Finding Light in the Darkness

Christina Callahan

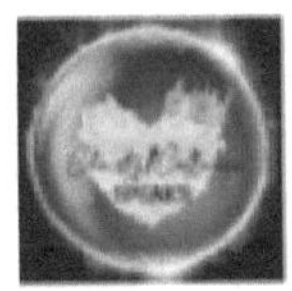

Table of Contents

"And we know that all things work together for good to those who love God, to those who are the called according to His purpose."
-Romans 8:28 (NKJV)
The Holy Bible: New King James Version.
Thomas Nelson, 1982

Preface

Life can be unpredictable. Everything feels fine one moment, and then your entire life spins out of control. For me, everything changed with a phone call—the type that shatters your world. On the other end was devastating news about my brother's life-threatening, head-on collision. That call was the moment my life unraveled, and I was thrust into a storm of dread, sleepless nights, and desperate prayers.

This book began as personal journal entries during some of the hardest moments of my life. *Writing was my way of processing the pain and searching for God's presence when everything felt impossible.* Something unexpected happened when I spilled my heart on the page. These notebook entries presented a story—one of hope and resilience—that I couldn't keep concealed. *I understood that the miracles I had witnessed were not only for me. They were intended to be shared.*

Glory Through Pain is more than my story. It's a testament to the beauty of faith and the undeniable evidence of God's miracles. Through my brother's long recovery, through my own heartbreak and exhaustion, I learned one thing over and over again: *God's timing is perfect, even when we don't understand it.*

My prayer is that this book encourages you to hold on to hope in your own struggles. *If you're drowning in grief, doubt, or the agony of waiting, I hope my story reminds you of this: God's love doesn't falter, and His grace is enough to carry you through.* In a broken world, miracles are still real.

May this book inspire you to see the extraordinary in the mundane and to believe, even in your darkest moments, that God is walking with you, working all things together for good.

Come along with me on this journey of faith, perseverance, and finding the miraculous in the midst of pain.

—Christy

1 Escape to the Forest

Reality

I never knew how tough a year could be until I almost lost both my dad and my brother. It started with Mom's panicked call.

"Your dad has a blood clot in his lung," she said, her voice trembling. *"The doctors gave him a 50-50 chance of surviving."*

"Fifty-fifty." The words echoed in my mind. It didn't feel real—couldn't be real. Mom didn't like to worry me. If she was saying this out loud, it had to be bad.

Weeks blurred by, like being in a fog. The day Dad got out of lung rehab? That felt like the first time in ages I could actually breathe. The sun poured into the living room, warming everything it touched. For a second, I let myself think—*maybe, just maybe, everything would be okay.*

And then the phone rang.

"Hey, Chris!" Dad's familiar voice crackled through the line, warm and steady.

"Daddy, how are you? How are your lungs?" I asked, trying to sound calm even as a tiny voice inside me screamed for reassurance.

"They're good. I'm good," he said, and I could hear the smile in his voice. *"But I really want to know how you are, sweetie pie."*

I smiled despite myself. That was just like Dad—always shifting the focus off himself.

"I've been coaching club volleyball," I said, trying to keep my voice even. *"But, Dad, I really want to know how you're doing."*

"I'm off the breathing machine now," he said with a chuckle. Then his tone softened. *"You know, Chris, I think it's this purple God bracelet you gave me—the one with John 3:16 on it. It feels like it protected me, like God's hand was there. I truly believe it helped me get through."*

Warmth flooded my chest, and for a moment, the world felt steady.

But then he took a sharp breath, and my stomach dropped.

"Chris, I have to go. I'll call you back." His voice was abruptly unsteady.

Minutes later, the phone rang again.

"Chris, I'm sorry about that," Dad said, but this time his voice was unsteady, quivering. *"That was the police. Your brother Duke was airlifted to Shock Trauma ICU. I have to go. I'll call you when I know more. Meet us at the hospital later at three o'clock."*

When Dad told me Duke was in Shock Trauma, the world felt like it had tilted. The walls around me seemed to close in, the air too thin, like I couldn't catch my breath. I clutched the phone so tightly my fingers ached, as if it were a lifeline.

Duke had faced so much already—schizophrenia had turned his world upside down. When he was on his medicine, though, you would have never known. Balanced and composed, he seemed just like anyone else. Before the accident, he didn't always take them like he should've, and that made everything harder. But this? *This was a new kind of fight.*

Terror exploded inside me, raw and consuming. My heart pounded so hard it felt like it might break free from my chest. Tears spilled down my cheeks as my mind raced.

'No. Not Duke. Not my little buddy.'

I was clinging desperately to the image of him as I'd last seen him—full of life, full of laughter. Duke, with his mop of messy blond hair and bright blue eyes that always seemed to sparkle, was the definition of joy. But that image blurred as another memory came rushing forward, unbidden but vivid.

Flashback

We were kids again, racing through the woods. I could feel the mud squishing beneath my sneakers, and heard the crunch of leaves underfoot. Duke's little legs wobbled as I chased him, both of us giggling like we'd had all the time in the world. Then he tripped, and the laughter stopped.

I ran to him, panic rising as I saw blood trickling from his tiny hand, pricked by a thorn. His face twisted in pain, tears streaming. But even then, there was bravery in his blue eyes—eyes so much like Dad's.

"Oh no, Duke! Are you okay?" I squealed, my own voice trembling.

Brushing his tears away, he wiped his bloody hand on his red athletic shorts and gave me a wobbly smile.

"Chwisty, I love you," he said softly, his small, dirt-covered hand reaching for mine as his tear-filled eyes sparkled with a quiet bravery.

My heart melted. I grinned back through my own tears. *"Whenever you're in trouble, just remember—I'm always here."*

He was fearless, racing headlong into life as if nothing could have stopped him. That memory lingered, refusing to disappear, a reminder of the youngster he once was. Duke wasn't the same small kid anymore, but he remained my brother. And now, more than ever, I wanted him to come through.

That courage, even in the smallest moments, was what I needed to hold onto now. But would it be enough?

That memory felt like a lifetime ago, but now, sitting here, it was impossible to ignore how far we'd come—and how much was still at stake.

Reality

Sitting there, on that couch, it hit me like a punch to the gut. Tears blurred my vision, and fear? It was like a weight on my chest. I tried to hold onto that moment—Duke's tiny hand reaching for mine—but now? It wasn't me he needed. *It was God.* And that thought? That thought had stung.

'*Jesus... I really have to trust You, don't I?*'

"*Jesus, please help us! Jesus, Jesus, please don't let him die!*" I cried out, my hands pressed against my face as I rocked back and forth, sobbing.

My breath came in ragged gasps as I pictured Duke's soul reaching out—not to me this time, but to God.

Their struggles forced me to confront my own faith—was I truly trusting God, or just hoping He'd come through?

'*He doesn't know You, Lord. But please, give him a chance. Please, let him be okay.*'

The weight of the unknown crushed me. I couldn't imagine a world without Duke—my brother, my best friend.

The thought of losing him tore through me, dragging me back to that helpless place I'd tried so hard to forget.

But there I was—vulnerable, raw, and desperate, with my heart wide open and afraid.

As I fervently prayed for Duke, my thoughts strayed to when I was a little child and had resorted to God. For the first time, I really realized what it meant to be in need of Him. My faith was formed at that moment, and after all those years, I was holding onto it more firmly than before.

This wasn't the first time fear had gripped my heart like that, and I found myself back in a memory I thought I'd forgotten...

2 The Call That Changed Everything

Flashback

I can still see myself as a 10-year-old girl, curled up in my mom's bed wearing my favorite pink-hearted nightgown, feeling safe and warm. But that safety shattered when I heard an anguished cry from downstairs. The sound sent a jolt of fear through me, and I pulled the pillow over my head, internally whispering, *"This is just a dream. This is just a dream."* But it wasn't.

My heart raced as I scrambled out of bed and crept down the stairs, an eerie feeling prickling at my skin. *Something was wrong—terribly wrong.* I reached the kitchen and froze.

"Mom, what happened?" I asked, my voice shaky and small.

Mom was pacing back and forth, clutching the cream-colored landline. Her face was tight with panic, her eyes darting around as if searching for answers in the air.

"Is he okay? Is he all right?" she cried into the receiver, her voice breaking with anger and desperation.

I felt the fear climb up my spine. *"Who isn't all right, Mommy?"* I asked, my heart pounding so loud I could barely hear my own voice.

She didn't answer right away, just kept pacing, clutching the phone like it was the only thing holding her together. Finally, after what felt like an eternity, she hung up.

"Honey, it's Daddy. He was shot in the stomach at work," she said, her voice trembling with fear.

She pulled me into a hug, and I felt the deep, liberating moan escape her chest. It was a sound I'd never heard before—a sound that made my stomach drop.

"Oh no, Mom," I whimpered, tears welling in my eyes. *"Is Daddy going to be okay?"*

Before she could answer, my two brothers appeared behind me. They'd heard everything.

"Mom! Is he okay?" they shouted in unison, their voices cracking with fear.

Mom took a deep breath and straightened her posture, forcing a brave face. *"He's in the hospital,"* she said firmly.

"I don't know yet, but I'll find out. Grandma is coming over to stay with you while I go see him. I'll call as soon as I know anything. I promise."

Her voice wavered, but she wouldn't let us see her crumble. *"For now, you all can stay home from school today. Go back to your rooms and get dressed before Grandma gets here."*

Dressed and waiting on the stairs, my thoughts turned to God—the God Mom and Dad had always taught us about. The God I'd believed in without question when I was little.

The last time I'd prayed to Him, I was about five years old, begging for a miracle to get back the pecan cinnamon rolls Mom had taken away as punishment. I'd gotten half of them back, and in my five-year-old heart, that felt like proof that God listened.

But this time? Totally different. This wasn't about candy or toys or anything I could fix with a smile. *This was about my dad. My dad.* And the fear? It sank into my bones. *This wasn't just a prayer—it had to mean something.*

I folded my hands and closed my eyes, the little girl in me whispering a desperate prayer: *"God, what happened to my dad? Will You save him?"*

That night, sitting on the stairs, I prayed like my whole world depended on it. I had no clue back then, but fear and faith would keep crashing into each other throughout my life. Years later, Dad told me about his own night—a night when everything could've ended, but somehow didn't.

That night wasn't just his; it was ours. It became the proof I didn't even realize I needed.

As I sat there, holding on to my prayer for dear life, I started to see it: fear and faith didn't cancel each other out. They walked side by side. And when I finally heard Dad's story, it showed me something I hadn't understood before—*God really is there, even when everything felt broken.*

3 Prayers Amid Gunfire

Flashback Continued

That November night started off like any other, just another shift for Dad at the Giant Food Store. He worked nights as a Special Police Officer, and nothing too tragic ever happened—until it did.

Before leaving for work, Dad took a moment to stand in the doorway, watching his family. The sound of my laughter echoed through the house, warm and light. Duke was on the floor, pretending to wrestle with Jeff, even though Jeff was five years older and a lot stronger. It made Dad smile.

It was these moments, quiet and simple, that made everything else seem less important. He watched his family, his heart swelling with pride. Duke, too young to understand, clung to Dad's leg, a silent plea for attention in his big blue eyes. Dad didn't mind. He'd always been the anchor. He'd promised his family, God willing, he'd always come home.

With a final look back, he grabbed his coat and headed out the door, stepping into the cold night.

"Be extra vigilant when Carl B. comes in," his boss had warned that evening, pointing toward the entrance with an edge in his voice. *"Do not let him get out that door. Got it?"*

Dad nodded, the weight of responsibility settling on his shoulders. He only had a vague description of Carl: restless, shifty, always up to no good. Just another night, right?

The store's hum remained constant, as did the gentle ringing of the register. However, there was something in the air that night. *Something was not right.*

Dad had been working so hard for that raise, but little did he know—his world was about to turn upside down.

Reality

For ten years, I'd prayed for Duke to be balanced mentally, to find peace, and to truly know God. Was his accident somehow the answer to those prayers—or just some cruel twist of misery from the Creator I loved so much?

The chaos of that night eventually faded, but the scars it left behind never did. I carried them, etched into my heart, even as life moved forward.

4 Echoes of Survival

Flashback

When I heard Dad tell that story, I experienced a shift in myself. It was the kind of story that made life feel fragile, precious, and awful all at once. Although, the fact that he survived did not make those events any less important. My entire being was imprinted with the fear and the near-death experience.

Even though the world continued to move on, the anguish from those moments lingered with me throughout the days. Somehow, I felt as though I was stuck in time.

The hurt from those moments clung to me as the days passed, though the world kept moving forward. Somehow, I felt stuck in time. Almost losing him wasn't something I could simply shake off—I could barely process such strong emotions at such a young age. As the days wore on, the pressure of those moments didn't fade. *You don't just put down the burden of nearly losing someone you love.* It lodged itself deep inside me, slipping into the unspoken spaces of my life like an unwelcome guest.

I think about that moment often—how close we came to losing Dad. It clings to me, raw and too vivid, even now. *Like a ghost you can't shake, no matter how much you want to.*

Even now, I can still hear the whir of the machines in that hospital room—the faint hum of Dad's heart, beating until it almost didn't. *That sound became a shadow, its weight clinging to those days and lingering even now.* But life doesn't stop for mourning. It doesn't pause, no matter how much your heart wants to stay frozen in time.

Reality

The bang of the front door jolted me from the memory.

"Hello, honey pig," Ben says, his voice warm as he steps inside.

"Honey pig?" I shoot back, but my lips betray me with a smile.

He crossed the room, pulling me to my feet before I can even think of a comeback. His hug was solid and grounding, like the world has stopped spinning for just a second. His puppy-soft eyes met mine, and I melted into him, taking in the mix of his cologne and something indefinably him—home.

His hand stroked my hair, and the words slipped out before I could stop them. *"I don't want you to let go."*

He tightened his hold, like he'd heard my soul whisper it. *"Never."*

For a moment, gratitude bubbled up so fiercely it almost spilled over. This man—this rock in the chaos—was mine.

But life, relentless as ever, tapped on my shoulder. *"What time is it?"* I ask, reluctantly stepping back.

Ben glanced at his watch. *"The right time to leave. It's 2:30—we need to go."*

The sunlight outside felt like an interrogation lamp, even through my sunglasses. I leaned back in the car, exhaustion pulled at me from every direction. Hours of crying, worrying, praying—they all have a way of hollowing you out.

5 Light in Fragile Moments

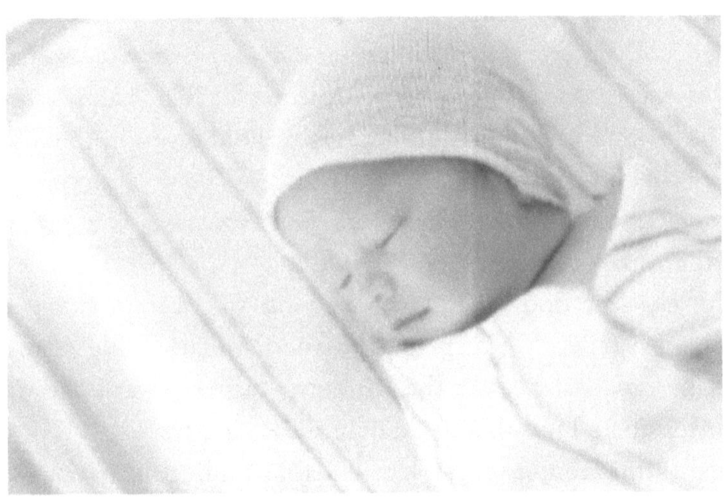

Reality

The familiar sounds of hospital elevators penetrated my chest. For all of life's insecurity and volatility, hospitals had always seemed like a strange kind of shelter to me. The place's steady pace felt reassuring, even calming. But the machines—those cold, constant beeps and whirs—always made me anxious. *They reminded me of how delicate things can be, and how close we were to losing hope.*

That fragile mix of optimism and anxiety followed me into the hospital. When we stepped through the enormous elevator doors, my breath caught. Even now, as I waited for news about Duke, the hospital didn't scare me. It was the waiting that pressed on my chest like a weight. The building itself, with its antiseptic air and steady hum of machines, felt more like a cocoon than a cage. But no amount of comfort in the surroundings could quiet the what-ifs racing through my mind.

Although hospitals had come to symbolize everything that could go wrong, Ben's hand in mine reminded me that not everything had to go wrong.

We walked side by side, the elevator looming in front of us like a giant, steel trap waiting to close. I took a deep breath and stepped in behind Ben, but the familiar, suffocating wave of claustrophobia hit me all at once. *It felt like the walls were closing in, pressing in tighter with every second.* My fingers instinctively reached for Ben's hand, squeezing it for some kind of comfort, something to hold on to in the midst of the overwhelming pressure.

"It's okay, babe. I'm here with you." Ben's voice was soft, grounding me in the chaos of my mind.

The elevator doors finally opened on the second floor, and I exhaled with relief. We turned right, the familiar feeling of urgency setting in as I dashed past the windows, racing toward the waiting room. And then, I was there—straight into Dad's arms.

Dad's arms around me felt like a lifeline, pulling me back to a time when everything felt easier—a time when I felt true joy. I could almost hear the sounds of laughter echoing in the background, the sunlight spilling through the windows of our family cabin, the gentle hum of life that wasn't all that complicated. Before the world settled on my chest, everything felt so heavy.

I snapped back to the present, the sterile smell of the hospital stinging my nose, and I looked at Dad. He continued to hold me, his arms firm yet soothing, dragging me away from the past, just enough to catch an eye full of his face. *It was like the present was pulling me back, saying, I need you here, don't get lost in the past.*

"Christy! We're so glad you're here!" he said, his voice thick with emotion.

But I couldn't help it. The past was beckoning me, as it always did when I stood on the brink of something hard. It was a reminder that there used to be a time when I didn't have to prepare myself for every piece of bad news that came my way. I didn't need to bear the weight of my worries on my shoulders.

I squeezed my eyes shut for a moment, and there I was, back to that moment—that moment when life felt a wee bit lighter, when everything hadn't gotten so damn complicated. I missed the carefree family moments at the cabin, before everything fell apart—before Dad's trauma turned pain into a constant companion.

As I sat there, my thoughts drifted to another hospital visit, one from years ago. Life felt heavy then too, but somehow, joy managed to find its way in.

6 Web of Hope

Flashback

I've learned that life doesn't come in neat chapters. Even as we celebrated Brittany's arrival, Dad's pain lingered—a quiet reminder that joy and hardship often walk hand in hand. Life wasn't done testing us—it never seemed to be. I've always felt this soft, aching sympathy for my dad and his back pain...

After being shot, it seemed like the world just dumped on him—pain worse than anything I could imagine. His doctor gave him pain medication, which turned into a mess of its own. Slowly, the pills started to take over. Not just his body, but his mood too. And the more he got into them, the more everything else seemed to spiral. The alcohol addiction, the arguments, the emotional wreckage—it was hard to watch.

I was just a kid, only 11 years old, and I'd hear them fighting in the next room. *'My dad's going to leave. He's going to leave us.'*

I'd lie awake at night, trying not to listen, but it was impossible. The fear of losing him was like a weight pressing down on me. To cope with the chaos, I found comfort in the simplest of things. *Space Jam* became my escape—Michael Jordan, flying through the air, dunking on everyone, like he could defy gravity. I wasn't great at basketball—let's be real, I was terrible—but I dreamed of soaring like him.

And R. Kelly's *"I Believe I Can Fly"* on repeat? Yeah, that became my personal anthem. I sang it loud, with all the conviction a kid could muster, even if I was still struggling with math homework. It was my way of pretending everything was okay, of imagining a world where pain didn't exist, and dreams didn't crash and burn. I was using it all to escape, but I didn't care. It felt good. *Sometimes, imagining was all I could do.*

Reality

Sitting in that hospital waiting room during Duke's surgery, fear gnawed at me like an old, unwelcome friend. The clock on the wall seemed to mock me with every agonizingly slow tick—each one a hammer pounding on my chest. *'Is he going to be okay?'*

Spinning in my head, the question wouldn't leave me alone. I walked in circles, trying to shake off the feeling, but the what-ifs stuck to my foot like gum, and I couldn't peel them off.

Back then, Duke was my rock—always steady, always there. But now, as I paced the hospital corridors, I prayed he could find the same strength for himself.

While I prayed Duke would get better, there was a glimmer of something familiar in me—hope. It reminded me of another time I'd held on to hope, when it seemed out of reach.

Flashback

I blinked, and suddenly I was back in that golden September morning. The air smelled like freshly cut grass, and sunlight poured through the windows, casting a warm glow that felt at odds with the heaviness in my dad's voice.

"Where are you going, Daddy?" I asked, rushing into his room to hug him before school.

He looked up, startled. *"Hey, Chris. I'm going to get some help to stop drinking. I never wanted it to be like this, Christy, but I just can't take the pain anymore.*" His voice cracked, and one lone tear rolled down his cheek.

I felt my heart shatter, once again.

I couldn't help it—I was a kid, and that moment felt too big for me to grasp. But then, I noticed the pink and green floral wallpaper behind him—something so innocent, so childish, it made me feel like I could handle this. *This is what you focus on when things are hard. Find something small to hold onto.*

I reached out, placing my hand on his shoulder, my voice trembling with hope. *"Daddy, I'm so thankful you're getting help. I've been praying for God to help you! Where are you going?"*

Tears streamed down our faces as we hugged. I didn't want to let go. The relief, the love, the tiny thread of hope—I wanted to cling to it, just for a little longer.

"I'm going to Father Martin Ashley's," he said, and it sounded like the answer to every prayer I'd ever whispered. *"It's one of the best places Mommy and I could find."*

We hugged tighter, rocking back and forth, and for just a second, I imagined, *Maybe everything is going to be okay.*

Reality

In an instant, all the warmth of the sun and the smell of freshly cut grass disappeared. The sound of my dad's voice faded, his tear-stained face remaining in front of me. It was as if I'd opened a window, and reality rushed in like a blast of cold air, waking me from the daydream. I was no longer a child, not in a sunny room. Now, I was pacing the clean, quiet hospital corridors, listening as the clock ticked, a drumbeat to my anxiety.

Finally, I walked to the front desk, my hands shaking so much.

"Excuse me, is there a status update on Duke Callahan? He's been in surgery for a long time." My voice cracked, betraying the panic I was trying so hard to keep under control.

The receptionist, Darrell, barely looked up, like he didn't see the tornado of worry swirling in my eyes. *"Let me check,"* he said, and in a calm tone that could've been in a documentary about How to Be Chill in the Midst of Chaos. He dialed the nurse. I stared at him like he was speaking in another language.

A minute later, he turned back. *"They just finished the surgery. They're moving him to room 225."*

225—the room number seemed to carry the weight of a thousand prayers. I nodded as I walked back to my family, trying not to let the tears spill. I felt the relief bubbling up. *'Okay, he made it. He's still here.'*

"He's out of surgery," I said, my voice probably sounding way more casual than I felt. *"We can go see him soon."*

Mom's face was a mix of relief and doubt, but she tried to smile. *"Phew."*

I nodded, swallowing the lump in my throat. It was a miracle. Even with Duke getting through the surgery, the weight of the moment—heavy, relentless—stayed with me.

Then, my mind started racing—again. *'Why did life have to be full of pain? Why couldn't we just feel okay all the time? Why couldn't God just take the hurt away?'*

These questions swirled in my head, relentless as always. I hated them. I hated that I could never get a solid answer, that I felt like I had to keep walking through life with these questions locked inside.

7 Finding my Rhythm

Reality

The questions from the waiting room still buzzed in my mind as I followed Ben into the hospital room.

As I glanced at Ben, I realized I wasn't walking this road alone. His presence was like an anchor in the storm, even if we were both barely holding it together. He didn't have to say anything—I could *feel* it. He was here, and so was I. Somehow, that had to be enough.

I followed Ben into the hospital room, my mind a blur of everything that had been happening. My heart was hammering, and my hands? Trembling like a leaf caught in a storm. But, of course, I tried to play it cool.

Ben plopped down in a seat, and I caught the way his shoulders were stiff, how his eyes refused to meet mine—like he was fighting the world to keep it all together. Oh, my sweet husband. I was so thankful that he was there with me, even if it felt like we were both teetering on the edge of some kind of emotional cliff.

I took a deep breath, trying to remind myself, for what felt like the hundredth time, that I had made it through worse. *Come on, Christy. You've handled adversity before.* I repeated it over and over silently, but my gut wasn't buying it.

Adversity. I don't know why, but that word always made me think of sports. Volleyball, in particular. Yeah, I guess my brain couldn't even sit still in a hospital waiting room without thinking about it.

I swallowed back tears as I took deep breaths, reflecting on the challenges I had faced so far in my life, where it was volleyball that gave me a sense of control. It was funny to me now that I still thought of it that way.

The waiting room's stark fluorescent lights pressed heavily on me, and my mind instinctively retreated to a place that had usually grounded me: the volleyball court. There, the rhythmic sound of the ball and the squeak of sneakers had been my sanctuary from life's chaos.

Flashback

Volleyball wasn't just a game; it was my constant. Regardless of the mayhem around me, the court was my safe haven—a place where I felt in control, even though the rest of my life was anything but.

I smiled at the thought even though it felt a little ridiculous. How many times had I found myself in situations where everything felt out of control, and volleyball was the thing that brought it all back? The volleyball court had always been the place where I could breathe, the place where I didn't have to worry about anything else. It was always there when the rest of my world was falling apart.

I thought back to those early moments, when everything clicked and I found my rhythm, when the chaos of anything else slipped away and the gym became my sanctuary.

By high school, I was beginning to understand—life was a rollercoaster. One minute you're flying with your hands in the air and you're like, *I've got this all figured out.* The next minute, you're sinking to the bottom and wondering whether you've been abandoned by every bit of joy you ever knew. But, oh, those highs. They felt so good. It was so sweet, it almost made the lows worth it.

When Dad got sober, things felt like they were almost right again. Not perfect, but better. Yeah, better. That should've been the theme of my teenage years: *"Slightly Better."* It was like trying to build a house out of sand—you didn't really know when it would all crumble, but you hoped it wouldn't. And I guess, if I'm being honest, I didn't expect it to.

High school? High school was a whole new world. And not the fun kind you read about in books. More like the kind where everything felt a little too small, a little too suffocating, and you had to wonder—*who thought brown brick walls without a single window was a good idea?* Fallston High looked like a prison. Thanks for that, universe.

But hey, volleyball. That was my escape. Even when I was sitting on the bench most of freshman year, volleyball was my thing. I could almost *feel* the ball in my hands. I could almost *taste* the victory. *Almost.*

Then came basketball. Oh, basketball. Nothing like watching your own panic attack unfold in real-time. Would I make the team? Probably not. Was I good enough? Probably not. But did that stop me? *Absolutely not.*

The night before basketball tryouts, I was out by the lamppost, practicing layups like some desperate, feverish mess. My brother Duke—sweet Duke—found me there.

"What are you doing out here so late?" he asked, his angelic blond hair practically glowing in the moonlight. I swear, it was like he had a halo.

"Hey, Duke! Can you show me how to do a layup?" I said, dribbling the ball back and forth like I was some kind of expert.

"Sure." He grinned, stepping into the light like he was auditioning for a role in an action movie.

He showed me the steps. Over and over. And somehow, by the end of it, I wasn't as terrible as I'd started.

"Wow, Duke! Thanks a million!" I said, like I was ready for the WNBA draft.

The next day? The tryout list. There, in big bold letters: *Christy Callahan.* I felt like I had just won the lottery: the fever, the exhaustion, the panic—all of it disappeared for a second. And that, my friends, was the beginning of my two-decade-long dramatic sports story.

Fast forward to high school, where my friends were forming cliques with their sports teams, and Tara, my bestie, was suddenly hanging out with the "cool" crowd. And me? Well, I was, once again, the outsider.

But you know what? Volleyball was still my refuge. Even if I spent more time on the bench than I cared to admit.

Then there was softball. Don't even get me started. When I didn't make the team, it felt like the universe just dropped a giant anvil on my head. I sat there, in the rain, sobbing like a total mess. Then, like she always did, Mom showed up.

"Chris, that's okay. You did two sports. That's enough," she said, her voice warm and steady like a balm on my raw nerves.

It helped. It did. Although, the sting still lingered.

Over time, though, I learned that trying—showing up—was what really mattered. And when all else fails, remember Psalm 139:14-15: *"I will praise you, for I am fearfully and wonderfully made."* I wasn't worthless. I wasn't anything less than enough. And that, my friends, was something I had to remind myself of over and over again.

As I sat there, reflecting on all the ways volleyball had grounded me, I realized that something much bigger had been happening all along—my faith was growing. It wasn't just about the game; it was about the inner strength faith was building within me. That growing faith gave me the courage to confront the chaos and rise above my insecurities.

Now, I tried my hardest to cling to that faith when it seemed like life was attempting to put me to the test again. Because sometimes having all the answers wasn't as crucial as holding on when everything else seemed to be crumbling.

8 Faith in the Shadows

Reality

My parents stood beside me, one on each side of my brother's hospital bed. There was an unsettling tension between them, but their unspoken communication said everything—shared glances and a silence heavy with what words couldn't express.

Everything in the air was heavy—a weight in their eyes, too difficult to describe and too deep to grasp. We stood there, staring at my brother, attached to machines, the constant beeping filling the room. That sound had always been maddening, and I hated it—*until then*. His face was still smeared with blood—a bloody reminder of how close we had come to losing him. It was too much. My chest felt as if it might split open from the weight of it all.

As the sterile scent of antiseptic filled my breath, I knelt next to him, my trembling hands clasped together. The moment weighed heavily on my chest, and every monitor beep served as a harsh reminder of how fleeting life can be.

I also could hear the rapid rhythm of my own heart. I prayed—not in sureness that everything would be okay, but in deep, raw, *how-can-this-be-happening* honesty, begging God to save my brother's life. The surgeries weren't finished, and I didn't know how to face the uncertainty.

Then, as I knelt there, a thought struck me. I thought of all the times I had doubted—wondered if God was even listening. I had questioned my faith like a child trying to hold onto a balloon, always wondering if I'd been grasping only air.

There had been so many moments when I questioned if I could still believe, when the world felt too big, too indifferent, to care about me. I had feared being forsaken. But in that moment, kneeling beside my brother, the enormity of it all felt different. I felt God's presence, soft but undeniable, surrounding me like a blanket. I was scared, but I wasn't alone.

I thought about how far He had carried me through the pain that almost destroyed me, the doubts that nearly drowned me. And yet, He had never left. Even when I couldn't see it, He had been there, guiding me through my questions and struggles.

All those years of wondering if I was enough, if my dreams would ever come true, didn't matter now. I wasn't perfect, I wasn't who I thought I'd be, but I was here, kneeling beside my brother, holding onto this fragile hope. I could feel it—God's love, messy and real, even in the doubt.

A new strength began to stir within me as I saw my brother hooked up to all that machinery. The doubts didn't disappear, but there was a glimmer of something I hadn't known I needed—hope, faith, and the sense that somehow, God was still moving, even if I couldn't see it clearly.

My knees dug into the cold floor, but I felt closer to Him than I had ever been before. Through the fear, through the uncertainty, I was starting to understand: God was there—not because I was perfect, not because I had it all together, but because He loved me in the mess and in the doubt, in the rawness of my humanity.

A new power simmered within me as I watched my brother, tangled in wires and tubes. The doubts didn't vanish, but I felt something I didn't know I was missing—a quiet certainty that, even if things didn't make sense, God was still at work. I prayed again, this time with a deeper understanding of my faith, not in perfection, but in raw honesty.

I swallowed back tears, taking deep breaths, reflecting on my life and how, at times, volleyball had given me a sense of control. It seemed funny now, how I still clung to it as something constant. But it was always there, even when I didn't have faith in anything else.

It was as if I were standing on the edge of something I couldn't yet define. The same uncertainty I'd carried for years was there, but now there was a quiet knowing—a shift, however small. Even if I couldn't see it, maybe God was still moving. *Maybe faith didn't have to be perfect to be real.*

Flashback

My parents always said I could do anything if I wanted to, but sometimes, it felt like they were the only ones who believed in me. Confidence? It was a butterfly—always fluttering out of reach. Sitting the bench in volleyball and basketball, getting cut from the softball team? Not exactly a sign of future athletic stardom. My childhood dreams of becoming an actress or a writer were starting to fade, like a half-forgotten movie script I couldn't quite remember. The weight of my self-doubt only grew heavier.

One morning in ninth grade, Mr. Tospin called our names for a group project. When I saw Jessie walk across the room to join the circle of popular kids, a knot twisted in my stomach. I wasn't a stranger to awkwardness, but this felt different. I sat with the group, feeling like I didn't belong.

"Hi," I said, my voice stumbling out.

"Hey, Christy," Jasmine replied, her tone flat.

Jessie—ugh, Jessie—was the worst. She wore black all the time and had this pendant that screamed *"I'm mysterious."* She wasn't shy about her beliefs either.

"I cast a spell on Jimmie," Jessie said with a smug grin, leaning back in her chair. "He's going to fall in love with me."

I stared at her, wide-eyed. "You what?"

"Yeah," she said, as if it was no big deal. "I cut my wrists and sprayed blood on the wall. It worked. Now he's in love with me."

My stomach churned. I wanted to say something, but the words stuck in my throat. Instead, I found myself staring at her pendant, the only thing about her that didn't terrify me. I didn't know much about Jesus then, but I knew He existed, and I clung to that.

"Aren't you afraid of dying?" I asked, tilting my head, trying to ignore the fear gnawing at me.

"I don't believe in life after death," Jessie said coldly. "Once we're dead, we're just dead. No heaven, no hell. Just nothing."

That thought rattled me. *What if she was right? What if there was no God, no afterlife?* The thought was too much to bear, so I shoved it away, but it still lingered.

For the next few months, those questions crept in like unwelcome guests, asking, *What's the point of living? Why bother?* I cried every day at school, and when I got home, I ran to the trampoline, hoping the sky would take away the pain.

One afternoon, I lay on the trampoline, my eyes blurry with tears. Everything felt too big—the sky, the grass, even the sun. It was all too much. Then, a voice cut through the fog of my thoughts.

"You okay?" Dad's voice cut through the quiet.

I jumped, startled. My mind was so lost, I wondered if God was speaking to me directly. "Whew, Dad! I thought that was God talking. You scared me!" I laughed, but it was hollow.

He didn't laugh. He smiled, and just sat next to me, solid and reassuring. "What's going on, honey?" he asked, his voice softer than usual.

"I'm literally crying," I said, my voice small. "I don't know what to believe anymore. What if God doesn't exist?"

His face softened even more, and without a word, he laid down on the trampoline. We lay back, staring at the sky—me tangled in doubt, and him firm in his faith.

"I know God exists," he said, breaking the silence. "He saved me after the accident. The doctors said it was a miracle. I survived because He was there."

His words washed over me, simple yet sure. Something in the certainty of his voice loosened the knot in my stomach. I turned to him, and a tear rolled down his cheek, catching the sunlight. A glimmer of hope.

"I hope," I whispered, but doubt still clung to me. "But the stuff they teach at school... about evolution... it makes me question everything. What if it's all just... nothing?"

Dad smiled, a steady, calm smile. "We'll talk to your mom about it," he said. "But for now, how about we visit Sister Mary at the church? She has a way of making sense of things."

That simple offer brought a glimmer of hope. Dad's unwavering faith reached out through the darkness, guiding me back toward the light.

9 Hope Through Brokenness

Reality

I sat across from Dad in his living room, thinking about how many times his faith had carried us through—his terrible injury, my uncertainties, and now Duke's battle for his life. But after everything we'd been through, that faith felt heavier today.

Normally, we'd be talking—small talk, at the very least. But today, neither of us seemed to know what to say.

The beige walls felt too plain, too blank, like they were reflecting the weight of everything unsaid. Dad's old clock ticked softly in the background, steady and quiet.

He reached for his lower back, his face twisting in pain as he squinted. Even now, all these years later, I could see the strain written across him—physical, emotional, spiritual. It was all there, etched into the lines on his face.

"I just can't believe this accident happened," Dad said finally, his voice low and hoarse.

I nodded, swallowing the lump in my throat. "I know."

He rubbed his hands together absentmindedly, his movements slow and deliberate. "God has carried me through a lot of things," he said, his voice breaking. "But this... this is hard."

I could feel his words pulling at me, draining my strength, but I held steady.

Sitting there, I couldn't help but think of Duke. He had been there for me during one of the toughest moments of my life—my battle with depression and heartbreak. Like Dad, his words inspired me. They reminded me that I was worth something special, even when I couldn't see it myself.

I glanced at my phone, refreshing Facebook to check for updates on Duke. Part of me had shut myself off from the world, but another part of me wanted everyone to know how much of a miracle this was.

I noticed that Mom had posted twice that day. My heart clenched. I didn't want to read the posts—I was afraid they might contain bad news.

Instead, I slowly read the words, *aching my soul each moment I read, but embracing his second chance at life.*

Mom's Facebook Posts:

Post 1:

"Prayers needed for my son, Duke. He was in a head-on collision with another vehicle and airlifted to the hospital. After the initial shock, he's already been through two surgeries.

First, his diaphragm ruptured and pushed into his chest cavity. Second, they had to repair his aorta. Today, he went in for back surgery because he broke several vertebrae. He also broke his ankle, his other ankle, and his jaw. He sustained multiple fractures in the temple area.

He is heavily sedated right now, but last night, he opened one eye just enough to peek at me as a tear rolled down his cheek... I love you, Duke, with all my heart.

Please pray for the other driver and their families. We have a long road ahead of us, and all your prayers, love, and support are deeply appreciated."

Post 2 (Later):

"Thank you for your kind words and prayers. Duke had a very successful back surgery today—six rods and pins. Although he was heavily sedated and couldn't open his eyes, the nurse was still able to help him move his legs and give a thumbs-up.

Truly, God is taking care of my Duke and has blessed all the surgical team members at Shock Trauma. I couldn't ask for better care."

Flashback

After everything that summer—Dad's faith, our conversations about God, and our talk about visiting Sister Mary—I wasn't sure if hope would stick. But I wanted it to.

When I finally opened up to my parents about my struggles with depression, they didn't react the way I thought they would. They didn't get angry or lecture me. Instead, I think they could sense how much I needed help.

They signed me up for John Carroll, a Catholic high school that wasn't exactly in our budget. Though, they were willing to make sacrifices because they believed it could make a difference.

Honestly, I think we were all desperate for me to find some answers—or at least some peace.

The summer before my sophomore year, I clung to the idea that John Carroll would be my lifeline. A school where people believed in God and eternity? That had to help me rebuild my faith. Anything to get away from the shadows that had been haunting me.

I spent that summer trying to push away the dark thoughts, clinging to small moments of joy. I hung out with Kelly, my fiery tomboy best friend from Fallston High basketball. Her goofy charm was the antidote I didn't know I needed.

One blistering hot day, we sat outside in the driveway, passing a basketball back and forth. My orange bikini top stuck to my back, and Kelly's red hair was tied up in a messy ponytail.

"I'm actually excited for John Carroll," I said, bouncing the ball lightly. "I mean, they talk about God there. Maybe it'll help me stop thinking so much."

Kelly caught the ball and grinned. "Thinking about what?"

I hesitated. "You know... life. Death. All the big stuff."

She dribbled the ball between her legs. "Oh, you mean like, what's the point of it all?"

"Yeah," I said quietly.

Kelly nodded and shrugged. "My psychologist told me something yesterday that might help you. She said if you ask a question that doesn't have an answer, you'll just keep spinning. Like, why's an apple red? It just is."

Her words hit me like a flash of clarity. *Maybe some things weren't meant to be understood. Maybe I didn't have to have all the answers.*

"That's actually... really helpful," I said, catching the ball as she tossed it back to me.

"Good," she said, standing up and stretching. "Now let's play."

Reality

In Dad's living room, my thoughts moved from past anguish to present hope.

Dad looked over at me, his blue eyes glossy with unshed tears. "You know," he said softly, "God's been good to me. He's carried me through a lot of things. And I believe He's carrying Duke right now too."

I nodded, my heart full of emotion. "I believe that too."

I glanced down at my hands, clasped tightly in my lap. The memories of that summer, of Kelly's advice, of my first steps toward rebuilding my faith—they all swirled together in my mind.

Sometimes, the questions still crept in. *Why does life have to hurt so much? Why do bad things happen?*

But Kelly's words stayed with me: *It just is.*

I didn't have all the answers. However, I didn't need them to trust that God was still at work.

As I sat with Dad, I realized life wasn't just about surviving the hard parts; it was about fighting through them.

Could I trust God to carry me, too? Or would that type of trust be beyond my comprehension?

I was thinking about Proverbs 3:5, which states, "Trust in the Lord with all your heart and lean not on your own understanding."

The hardest part, though, was relying on Him when I didn't know everything and when life seemed like a complicated web of questions that I couldn't figure out.

Could I let go of my need for control and my fear and have faith that God would provide for me in the midst of uncertainty?

Weighty and unanswered, the questions lingered. Somewhere in the uncertainty, a subtle hope sprang, pushing me to hold on for whatever lay ahead.

10 Trusting God in the Silence

Reality

As we sat in Dad's living room, he stared into his drink, lost in thought, his face unreadable. It was the kind of stillness that felt heavier than any words we could've spoken.

I thought about how quickly everything could change. How one decision, one second, could flip everything upside down.

"Trust in the Lord with all your heart and lean not on your own understanding..." kept echoing in my head, like it was trying to break through.

How could I trust a God who'd let all this pain hang around? Who didn't stop my parents from falling apart? Who didn't take away Dad's pain, the same pain that pulled him back to the bottle over and over?

I wanted answers, but the more I asked, the more I felt myself unraveling.

Then, with a twist in my chest, I realized something. I saw God the same way I saw my dad—like a Father I couldn't trust. I loved them both, but the trust? That was gone.

But even sitting there, in that heavy silence with Dad, I noticed something else—something faint, something I couldn't quite put my finger on. Even in the brokenness, I felt like He hadn't abandoned us.

Maybe that's why I was still asking questions and still searching for peace.

It was like asking why an apple was red. *It just was.*

That hit me harder than I thought it would. My questions about God, life, everything—it was like someone had handed me a flashlight in a pitch-black room. Just enough light to see that maybe there was something bigger than the darkness. Bigger than the pain.

Although, even as the light flickered, the shadows crept back.

Flashback

My mind twirled back to junior year of high school, and the darkness started creeping back again.

One day, I walked into the cafeteria, head down, drowning in self-doubt. I went to Liz's table, where she sat with a group of soccer girls, my heart pounding, like it might just burst out of my chest.

"Hey, Liz. Did you save me a seat?" I asked, barely loud enough for myself to hear.

She glanced up. "No, there's no room left," she said, voice flat, turning back to her friends.

She wasn't lying—there wasn't any room. The sting of rejection cut deep. I swallowed hard, throat tight, and walked out, like my life depended on it. Skipped lunch. Ran to the library. Tears already falling.

I found a quiet spot behind a bookshelf, curled up into myself, and let the tears fall.

"Christy, are you okay?"

It was Sam. Her red hair and kind blue eyes looking at me, like she might actually care.

"No," I sniffled, wiping my nose on my sleeve. "I just feel like nobody cares. Liz didn't save me a seat, and I don't know why. I just want friends."

She smiled softly and sat down. "Well, I'll sit with you. Let's go eat lunch together."

That small act of kindness cracked through the loneliness. Sam became my rock. My best friend.

Although even then, the battle wasn't over.

One desperate Friday, I found myself standing on a chair in the kitchen, reaching for Dad's old antidepressants. I swallowed a pill, hoping it would magically fix me. Make everything stop spinning.

Mom walked in just as I was stepping down.

"Why is the chair there?" she asked, her voice sharp, eyes suspicious.

I froze. "I... I just took one of Dad's antidepressant pills. I'm sorry, Mom. I don't feel happy, and I thought maybe..."

Her face softened, and she pulled me into a hug. "Honey, you don't have to do this alone. Let's get you the right help, okay?"

And that was the turning point. Therapy, the right meds—it all started to change. For the first time, I didn't feel broken. I felt human.

By senior year, I could finally see a light at the end of the tunnel.

As graduation came closer, Matthew 11:28 kept echoing in my mind: *"Come to Me, all you who labor and are heavy laden, and I will give you rest."*

That verse became my anchor. Faith, family, friends—they reminded me that help exists, even in the darkest moments.

I didn't know what came next, but there was this quiet voice telling me to hold on. Maybe this wasn't the end. But it felt like standing at the edge of a cliff, not knowing if I should jump or pull back.

11 Broken to Beloved

Reality

It began with the sound of sterile white walls surrounding me, the beeping of machines, the quiet whir of the hospital humming with life. I sat beside Duke, my brother, watching the shallow, labored breaths he took. His body was worn down from 28 surgeries, hours spent fighting for his life. The heaviness of it would not be ignored.

I glanced at Duke, his face pale, eyes closed. The beeping from the machines punctuated the silence, and my heart twisted at how small and fragile he looked.

"This can't be real," I whispered under my breath, eyes glued to him.

The nurse came in to adjust his IV, glancing at me with a soft but knowing expression.

"He's a fighter," she said quietly, almost too quietly, like she didn't want to disturb the fragile peace around us.

The truth was undeniable. He *was* fighting. And it hit me like a ton of bricks—life felt so fleeting.

I'd spent so long pretending I had it all together, but in that room, with Duke fighting for every breath, the truth hit me: I needed to change. I couldn't pretend anymore. Not to him, not to myself.

It wasn't just the noise of parties and distractions I had drowned myself in for so long—the late nights, the meaningless chatter—it was the *void* inside of me. The one I had been running from. Now, it was inescapable.

I reached out and gently squeezed Duke's hand.

"I'm here," I murmured, though I knew he couldn't hear me. *"I'm not running anymore. Not from you, not from me...not from Him."*

In that stillness, I realized that I needed something more than what I had been living for. Something that lasted. Something that could fill me, instead of leaving me emptier.

Sitting next to Duke, I experienced a familiar ache in my chest, the kind that results from trying to improve situations that I was unable to.

I closed my eyes and held his hand, his warm but brittle fingers a stark reminder of what he had been through. Tears blurred my vision as I choked out a whisper: *"God, I don't know what to do."*

Duke wasn't just my brother—he was *my person,* the one who got me in a way so much of the world never could.

In addition to accepting me, he embraced my silly personality, sense of humor, and interesting opinions. Every time I said something silly, like how fluffy guinea pigs were my favorite animal or whined dramatically about the minor irritations of life, Duke would laugh—deep, real laughter that rocked his shoulders and made him smile the happiest of such.

"You're one of a kind, Christy," he'd say, shaking his head like he couldn't believe how ridiculous I was. With him, I didn't feel like I had to tone it down or explain myself. He just *got it.* He got *me.*

As I sat here now, watching him fight to stay, the boundaries of my reality started to haze. The idea of living without him was unbearable.

Who else would laugh with me in chaos? Who else would roll their eyes in the perfect way when I went all drama queen?

Duke not only loved me, he *understood* me. The idea of losing that made me feel as though I was losing a piece of who I was. I had this soul connection with Duke like he was my twin at birth.

"God," I whispered again, holding his hand tighter, *"please. Don't take him yet. I'm not ready to let go."*

Flashback

That thought haunted me for days, dragging me back to when everything had first changed.

Back to that moment in college when I'd first turned to God after the wreckage of my first love. I had convinced myself that the new distractions—late nights, wild parties, endless noise—could drown out the emptiness.

But they didn't. *Nothing* did.

I went to a friend's brother's funeral one day after he sadly died in a vehicle accident. To provide my support, I wanted to be present. The service was held at a non-denominational, grace-filled church, which I had never been to before. I had no idea that moment would alter not just my life but also my eternity.

I could still see it clearly in my mind: the bright yellow lobby, the walls too bright, too clean. I clutched my purse tightly, anxiety gnawing at me, as I stepped into a room full of strangers. They were singing, arms raised, as if they were connected to something I couldn't see.

The music wrapped around me, a gravitational pull. It felt... *alive.* So much louder than the music I was used to, so much more vibrant than anything I had ever known. I didn't know the words to the songs, but I sang along anyway, feeling more like an outsider than part of something.

I could hear the soft, comforting voice of the pastor rising over the music. Gray-haired, steady—he had this presence that made everything seem more important.

"God loves you," he said, his voice like a steady heartbeat in the chaos of my mind.

Then he asked the question that sent a wave of fear and something else—something I couldn't name—crashing through me.

He continued, his voice steady but full of urgency, *"Would you raise your hand if you want to make Jesus the Lord of your life?"*

I froze. Tears sprang to my eyes, and my heart pounded in my chest. Slowly, without really thinking, I raised my hand. My fingers trembled, but I couldn't ignore what was stirring inside of me. Something bigger than my fear. Something bigger than me.

Could God forgive me? Would He really?

A gallant usher, noticing the tremor in my hands, pressed a simple gift into my palm. A pen, a small Bible, and a note of encouragement. It was small, it was simple, but in that moment, it felt like pure gold.

The pastor's voice cut through the room again, clear and firm: *"Repent for your sins to be made new."*

Jesus had died for me. He had already taken my brokenness, my guilt, and wiped it clean. All I had to do was accept the truth, pray, and repent, and God would change me from the inside out.

As the pastor's words echoed in the room, the verse he was preaching on, John 14:16, surged into my mind with the force of a freight train: *"And I will pray the Father, and He will give you another Helper, that He may abide with you forever."*

The Holy Spirit. This Comforter, this Helper who would stay with me always—a safety net in the chaos. I couldn't hold back the tears. I had no idea what came next for me, but something deep inside was shifting.

Bit by bit, I started to change. For the first time in my life, I felt *convicted.* I felt *guilty*—guilty for how I had hurt others, for things I wasn't proud of. I had been chasing everything except the right things. I had filled my life with distractions, but *nothing* had filled me.

I realized that the only thing that could fill me was God's love.

Everything I once thought was fun or exciting felt... *empty*. I had been heading down a road that pulled me away from the truth, but that was changing now.

A new life—one based on honesty, purpose, and faith—began to feel possible. It terrified me. Although, it also gave me hope.

I couldn't stop thinking about what it meant to live for Christ. For so long, I had thought He was angry with me, punishing me for my mistakes, for my failures.

That wasn't the truth. *He loved me, messy and all, and He forgave me.* John 3:16 had become more than just a verse. It was the truth that I could hold onto now: *"For God so loved the world that He gave His only begotten Son, that whoever believes in Him should not perish but have everlasting life."*

I wanted that. I needed that. And now, I knew without a doubt: *God loved me, no matter what.*

I stood in the empty gym, the volleyball court before me. My senior year was behind me—filled with triumphs and failures, victories and defeats. It had been chaotic, maddening, painful at times.

Now, looking back, I saw how each moment had been shaping me. I didn't know it then, but God had been preparing me all along, even when I couldn't see it.

All the pain, the struggles, the disappointments—they hadn't been for nothing. They had all led me there.

One thing was clear as I stood on the brink of what was to come: I had changed since I had first set foot on that college campus that year. I wasn't alone this time, and I hoped to be prepared for whatever came next.

But was I?

12 The Fight Within

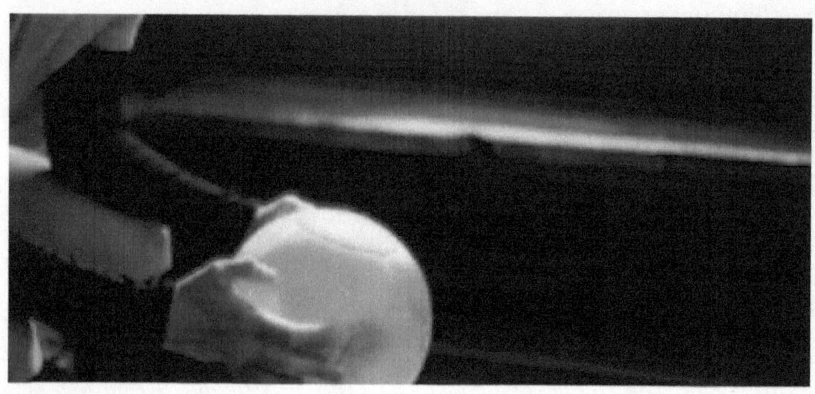

Reality

The first thing I noticed was the beeping. That deafening, constant roar that prevents all other thought. The computers seemed to be alerting me that Duke was barely alive and challenging me to ignore them.

I sat there gripping the icy metal armrests of the world's most uncomfortable chair. *Really—did they make these things on purpose to make you feel worse?*

I shivered and kept shifting, trying to find a position that wouldn't make my back feel like it was going to fail. No luck.

The air felt cold—too cold. Even Duke looked cold—lying there under those pitifully thin hospital blankets.

His face was pale, almost ghostly, and his chest rose and fell in these shallow, uneven breaths that made my stomach do weird flips. Not the fun, roller-coaster kind, either—the bad kind—like I was going to be sick.

"This can't be real," I whispered, my voice cracking.

The words weren't for anyone else. They were for me, and honestly, they didn't even feel big enough for the moment.

The nurse walked in, her pink scrubs a welcome splash of color in the otherwise dreary hospital room. Normally, pink is my happy color—it makes me think of sunsets and bubblegum and all things soft and cheerful—but here, it felt out of place. Not in a bad way, though. More like a reminder that the world outside still had light in it, even if this room didn't.

She moved with that quiet, practiced ease nurses have, like she could adjust an IV and sense my emotional unraveling at the same time. Her hands were steady. There was something gentle in the way she handled everything, like even the machines deserved her care.

Then her eyes met mine, and I saw it—the look. That soft, understanding gaze nurses seem to have perfected, the one that says, *I've seen a lot, and I know this is hard, but you're not alone.*

"He's a fighter," she said, her voice quiet but firm, as if she was reminding me of something I already knew.

And she was right. Duke *was* a fighter. Through 28 surgeries, through pain I couldn't even imagine, he had held on. And I knew he wasn't going to give up now.

I nodded, forcing a small smile that felt a little more real this time. *"Yeah,"* I whispered. *"He really is."*

I stared at Duke, willing him to move: to open his eyes, to do something. My mind was spinning, looking for anything to hold onto, and somehow it landed on volleyball. Because obviously, when your brother is fighting for his life, *that's* what you think about, right?

Flashback

The sound of sneakers squeaking on polished wood came rushing back. It drowned out the cheers of the crowd. I was on the bench, clapping when I was supposed to, plastering on a smile that felt like a lie. The court felt like another world, one I could see but never really touch.

Why am I even here? The thought was bitter and sharp, cutting through everything else. I gripped the edge of the bench, watching my teammates dive and spike and celebrate. They looked so alive, so in the moment, while I sat there, invisible.

The bus rides home weren't much better. I stared out the window, watching trees blur by while doubts circled in my head like vultures. *Stuck.* That's how I felt—moving but not really going anywhere.

Then there was that rainy Sunday in Southern Maryland. Another tournament, another game I didn't play.

I stepped outside, the rain hammering down so hard it soaked through my hoodie in seconds. I climbed into my car, gripping the steering wheel so tightly my knuckles turned white.

God, just give me a break, I begged inside.

It wasn't fancy. But it was real.

Months later, the answer came. Not in some big, dramatic moment, but in Coach Dennis.

"Christy, get in there," he said one practice, tossing me the ball like he was giving me no choice.

I fumbled, of course—because nerves—but his voice didn't waver. *"I know you've got this."*

Something about the way he said it made me believe him. For the first time, I felt seen. Not invisible.

It wasn't just about volleyball. It was about knowing I mattered—that someone believed in me even when I didn't believe in myself. That moment wasn't just a shift on the court; it was the first crack in the walls I'd built around myself.

Reality

The sound of Duke's shallow breathing pulled me back, cutting through the haze of memory. I blinked, the volleyball court fading into the sterile walls of the hospital room.

Now it was Duke who needed reminding. Maybe he couldn't hear me, but I needed to be steady—for him, if not for myself.

I reached out, brushing a strand of hair off his forehead. My hand trembled, but I didn't care. *"I'm here,"* I whispered.

For so long, I'd pretended to have it all together. Sitting there, watching Duke fight for every breath, it was painfully clear: I didn't. Not for him. Not for myself.

"I want to pray for you... will you let me?" I asked, respectfully.

Then, I waited.

Each second stretched out like forever. I held my breath without even realizing it. Then, it happened—a faint twitch.

His hand moved, barely, but it was enough to make my heart leap. He pointed to the paper, trembling, and slowly wrote a shaky *"YES."*

He had to write it down because he had just gone under jaw surgery and was healing. Tears filled my eyes, spilling over before I could stop them. For once, I didn't even try.

"Thank you, God," I whispered.

For the first time in a long time, I let out a deep, steady breath.

"It's like starting over," Duke said one day, his voice steady yet quiet, as if he was telling me a secret he was still discovering. He paused, staring down at his hands, which were covered in scars and swelling that told the story of everything he had gone through.

"But Chris, I'm just... thankful to even have the chance, you know?" He continued, looking up at me with those honest eyes of his. *"A lot of people don't get this—they don't get to try again. But I do. And I'm not going to waste it."*

His words weren't dramatic or rehearsed; they were raw and real, spoken like a man who had wrestled with the weight of everything he'd lost and somehow found gratitude in the fight.

Even in the hard moments, when frustration or pain took over, that thankfulness always surfaced. It was there in the quiet thank-yous he gave every nurse who came by, in the way he talked about the doctors who had patched him up like they were miracle workers.

Duke wasn't just clawing his way back; he was *grateful* for every inch he gained. And somehow, watching him made me grateful, too—not just for him, but for the quiet lessons he didn't even realize he was teaching me.

My thoughts were racing as I reclined in the most uncomfortable recliner in the world.

I couldn't stop thinking about the nurse's comment: *"He's a fighter."* She was correct. Duke was a fighter at heart. I was pleased by his fighting style, though, which was composed, comedic, and devoid of dramatic or loud claims.

That thought followed me out of the room, wrapping around me like a blanket—warm, steady, and unshakable. It wasn't about fighting through chaos or drama anymore. It was about something deeper, quieter, and infinitely stronger.

I realized that through this, God was showing me how He wanted me to fight too.

13 A Taste of Escape

Reality

I walked into Duke's room, the sterile, hospital-white walls surrounding me, always making everything feel too quiet. Too still. He was propped up in the bed, looking worn-out but somehow determined, that familiar *"I'm too tough to let this get me down"* look etched on his face.

"Hey, how's it going, champ?" I asked, trying to keep my tone upbeat, though the worry crept in.

He groaned and shifted slightly under the blankets.

A weak smile tugged at his lips. *"Well, you know, they wouldn't give me any water."*

I raised an eyebrow. *"What do you mean, they wouldn't give you water? Are you serious?"*

"Yup," he rasped, his voice rough like he'd been talking nonstop. *"I begged for it. But they told me I had to wait. So, I figured, why not help myself?"*

I stared at him, trying to figure it out. Then it clicked. *"Wait—did you try to get out of bed again?"*

He grinned. *"Maybe. Just a little. I threw my leg over the side like I was making a break for it. Had a whole escape plan in mind."*

I gasped. *"You tried to run? With your leg in a cast?"*

"Of course. Gotta fight for what you want, right?" He shrugged, nonchalantly, like he hadn't just risked his life for a sip of water. *"But yeah, my leg wasn't as fast as I thought."*

I laughed out loud. *"You were trying to run away for water?"*

"Exactly!" He chuckled, clearly proud of his failed escape. *"And guess what? The nurse caught me before I even made it two steps."*

I shook my head, giggling. *"Duke, you're hilarious. What were you planning to do at the water cooler—bust out a breakdance too?"*

He threw a pillow at me, a mischievous glint in his eyes. *"Hey, I'm thirsty! They've got this nature show on with fountains, rivers, lakes, oceans—"*

"Wait, what?" I interrupted.

"Yeah! It's like water torture. I can't even touch a drop of it because of the jaw surgery, and they're just parading all this beautiful water in front of me on the TV!"

I took a moment to process. Here was Duke, in a hospital bed with a leg in a cast, plotting an escape to the oasis of his imagination. It was mysteriously hysterical—and I couldn't help but laugh.

"So, basically, you're stuck in a water fountain documentary and the nurse's evil clutches?" I asked.

"Exactly! It's cruel," he said dramatically. *"And now I'm a water-crazed maniac to them."*

I laughed again, unable to hold it in. Only Duke could turn a hospital bed, a water quest, and a nature show into something both ridiculous and comforting.

Duke's antics reminded me—*life wasn't just about surviving the hard parts; it was about fighting through them, with humor, even in the most absurd ways.*

It was a reminder—whatever life threw at him, Duke would battle it with everything he had. Although, here he was, beaming at me as if nothing had happened.

I couldn't help but flash back to the moments when I had also wanted to run away from myself, the times when my own demons were overwhelming.

Duke's escape shenanigans reminded me of the times I'd wanted to run away—not from nurses, but from myself.

Flashback

The hip-hop beat pounded in my chest, loud and relentless, just like my entire life. I stood among a sea of strangers. Neon lights flickered, casting everything in a surreal, distorted glow. I wasn't even sure why I was there—maybe I was trying to fill some void I didn't want to admit existed, especially as a born-again Christian.

This wasn't my scene. The clinking glasses, the chaotic energy—it all blurred into a fog that felt more hollow than alive.

Was this a sign I needed to pray more? Did I need more time with God?

And then I saw him.

Billy leaned against the wall, arms crossed. His face was calm, detached—like he was untouchable. He wasn't trying to fit in—he didn't need to. He stood there, completely still, like he was anchored in a way no one else in that room could be. It was magnetic, and I couldn't look away.

"Not really the party type, huh?" The words escaped before I could think about them, my voice shaky but determined.

He glanced at me, barely moving, his dark eyes steady. His lips curved into the faintest smirk—not friendly, not unkind, just... knowing.

"The party isn't why I'm here," he said, his voice low and even, like the words had all the weight in the world.

I should've walked away. That was the moment. However, I didn't. Something about him held me there, even though my brain was screaming, *Run, Christy. Run.*

Why is it that the things you know are bad for you are always the most tempting? Like the pull of this man—his confidence, his quiet intensity—it was irresistible, and I hated how much I liked it.

He was trouble; I knew it already. And yet, there I was, standing too close, leaning in like he was offering me something I couldn't get anywhere else.

That was Billy. Trouble wrapped in a beautiful package. The kind of guy who didn't have to try to be dangerous—it just oozed off of him. And somehow, I wasn't running away. I was leaning into it, knowing full well I shouldn't.

Why did temptation always feel like that? Like everything I shouldn't have wanted was handed to me on a silver platter, impossible to ignore?

It wasn't long before those late-night conversations turned into long drives, windows down, his hand on the wheel, a cigarette dangling from his lips. He talked about the world like it owed him something, and maybe it did. Or maybe he was just really good at convincing me it did.

And then there was me.

Looking at him like he was a way out, like he was the answer to something I couldn't even put into words.

"Let's just go," I said one night, sitting cross-legged on the floor, a crumpled road map spread out between us.

My heart was pounding; the idea of escape lit me up from the inside. *"California. We could start over. Leave all this behind."*

Billy leaned back, his arms stretched out behind him, that slow, crooked smile spreading across his face. *"You're serious?"*

I nodded, the excitement almost too much. *"Yeah. Why not?"*

He looked at me for a long moment, like he was sizing me up, and then he shrugged. *"California it is."*

And just like that, it was set. The thrill of the idea was too good to question, too big to let doubt creep in. He made it feel like a real plan, like we could actually do it. Like I could have run away and finally found whatever I had been searching for my whole life.

As the miles ticked by and California got closer, the doubts started whispering in the back of my mind. *Why did he make this feel so easy? Why did the bad choices always come wrapped in something so irresistible?*

I shoved the thoughts down, holding on to the dream. For now, it was enough to believe in the escape, to think we could make something better of ourselves, even if part of me knew I was walking into another mistake.

With Billy, it felt like the kind of mistake you'd make twice. Maybe even three times.

Reality

Billy wasn't some pivotal figure in my story. He was a fleeting distraction, a reminder of all the times I'd tried to find meaning in the wrong places.

Now, sitting next to Duke, watching him fight for his life, I understood—I wasn't looking for an escape anymore. I was staying. For him, for me, for whatever came next.

14 Not Meant to Be Alone

Reality

I nudged the hospital door open, the familiar scent of antiseptic hit me like a slap. It was too clean—too clinical. Still, it was comforting in a strange way, like a reminder of simpler times when a scraped knee or a few stitches were the worst of it.

Then I saw Duke.

He was swallowed by bandages—his arms, legs, and even his neck tightly wrapped. His face, a mess of scabs and dried blood, looked like someone had taken a bat to the old Duke. When he turned to face me, slow and careful, my stomach twisted.

"Hey," I said, trying to sound casual, but my voice wavered, betraying me. *"You hanging in there?"*

He managed a weak half-smile, his voice barely above a rasp. *"Barely,"* he said. *"But I'll make it."*

That's when I noticed the stuffed lion Aunt Kay had sent, sitting perched on his pillow. Its fuzzy mane was massive, and its eyes seemed to follow me as I moved. Duke, the guy who always rolled his eyes at anything cute, now had a stuffed animal guarding him. It was ridiculous and strangely endearing.

"So, you're starting a stuffed animal collection now?" I teased.

His eyes flicked to the lion, and for a split second, his lips twitched in a faint grin. *"If it keeps Aunt Kay happy, I'll deal with it,"* he said, the laughter rasping out weakly.

It wasn't much, but hearing him laugh—even that tiny sound—was enough to loosen something in my chest. I noticed how stiff his neck was. Every tiny movement seemed to take an eternity, and it made me realize how fragile he looked now. I wanted to ask if he needed help propping himself up, but I knew better.

Instead, I just said, *"Wow! You can even turn your neck, or is that too difficult?"*

He grimaced in his neck cast and let out a half-laugh. *"It feels like my neck's stuck in concrete. But hey, I'm breathing, so that's progress."*

Mom walked in just then, her tired face softening as she assessed the scene.

"How's he doing?" she asked, scanning both of us with the sharp, calculating eyes of someone used to being the emotional anchor.

"He's got a stuffed lion now," I said, trying to keep it light.

Mom didn't smile, but the corners of her mouth softened. She stepped closer to Duke. *"You're taking your meds, right? Nurses are staying on you about that?"*

He tensed, avoiding her gaze. *"Yeah... it's just a lot."*

Her face hardened, but there was that familiar mom tone—equal parts concern and, *"you better do this. It's a blessing, Duke. Don't throw it away."*

He looked away, like if he couldn't see us, maybe this wouldn't be real. His voice barely rose above a whisper. *"I know. I just... didn't want to think it was real."*

"You're not alone," I said, sitting down next to him. I tried to keep my voice steady, not letting the lump in my throat break through. *"We're here."*

For the first time in what felt like forever, Duke's angry walls from the schizophrenia had come down. Turns out, he was actually taking the meds the nurses gave him—just like they'd been telling him to all along. It was the answer to a ten-year prayer, though not in the way I'd imagined.

The fight in him was still there, though. What replaced it was something else... exhaustion, thirst, and gratitude. It was like he finally realized—maybe for the first time—that he didn't have to carry it all on his own, and that life was still worth living.

I picked up the lion and fiddled with its ridiculous mane. *"Also, you've got a roommate now. A lion with creepy eyeballs. It's better than nothing, right?"*

Duke let out a short laugh, crackly in his throat. Although, it was enough. Even wrapped up like a mummy, wincing with every breath, Duke was still Duke.

His voice was a little gruff as he said, *"I... appreciate this. Thanks, but I know I can be a pain."*

I blinked, caught off guard. Duke didn't say stuff like that.

"You're not a pain," I said, my voice trembling. *"We're family."*

He shut his eyes for a moment, letting my words sink in. It felt small, but like a shift. Maybe this time, Duke would stop pushing us away.

"Yeah," he murmured, voice softer now. *"I don't know what I'd do without you guys."*

It was quiet after that, just the hum of machines in the background. It wasn't uncomfortable. It felt like real progress.

I left Duke's room a while later, that antiseptic smell clinging to my shirt like it wanted to follow me home. As I walked down the corridor, this wave of déjà vu smacked me—like I'd been in another room, another time, feeling the same wrench in my stomach.

Suddenly, Billy came rushing back into my mind, and I remembered how it all ended, years ago.

Flashback

I didn't need him to say anything. The silence was thick enough. It hung between us, pressing down like the air before a storm. He stood there, arms crossed, staring at the floor as if it held all the answers. I could practically hear the excuses swirling in his head, but I wasn't having it.

I felt like I was suffocating. I didn't even know where to start—maybe with the lies, maybe with how everything was falling apart in slow motion. I had enough space to be angry, but I was too tired for that now. It wasn't about the words anymore.

"You didn't mean to cheat on me," I said, my voice cracking more than I wanted it to. *"We moved all the way to California to leave that behind, to start fresh."*

He barely looked up, just a flicker of his eyes before they dropped back to the floor, as if it could somehow offer an escape from this mess.

"I didn't," he whispered, like he believed it.

Hearing him spew those lies made my blood boil. *Bullshit,* I thought. He kept trying to argue his way out of it while we stood amid the ruins of everything we once were.

I shook my head, frustrated. *"Billy, how many times are you going to say that? How many times are you going to 'not mean it' before you actually stop?"*

His jaw tightened, his fists clenching at his sides. There was nothing else to say, was there? His silence was louder than any words he could've spoken.

I watched him pack his things, every movement slow, deliberate, like he was trying to make it hurt less—but it didn't work. When he left, I didn't try to stop him. What was the point? He was already gone, even if his body was still standing there.

I just stood there looking at the empty spot where he had been when the door slammed behind him. It was as though someone had sucked the oxygen out of the apartment. Not a sound. No mayhem. Just the silence and me alone.

I wanted to scream, but I didn't have the energy. Instead, I sank into the couch, staring at the walls, and wondered who the hell I was without him.

It hit me then—I'd gotten so tangled up in him, I didn't know where I ended and he began.

The silence stretched on, and all I could hear was the echo of his words bouncing around in my head. *"I didn't mean for it to happen."*

"Well, guess what, Billy? You did." And now everything was different, and I had no idea how to fix it.

Reality

I blinked back to the present, standing in the hospital hallway. It hit me how both Duke's struggles now and Billy's betrayal back then had broken me open in different ways—both reminding me that none of us were ever meant to do this life alone. We can't hold it all together by ourselves, not when life gets real.

As I rubbed my eyes in an attempt to relieve the pressure, I heard footsteps coming. I turned to see Brittany, her ocean-blue, honest eyes greeting mine, her blonde hair striking the light.

"Hey," she replied in a soft, kind voice that seemed to soothe anything. *"How's Duke?"*

I didn't have the words for it. I didn't have the energy for the words. So I just shrugged. *"Still fighting."*

She didn't say anything right away, but I could see it in her eyes—she knew there was more I wasn't saying. She didn't push. Instead, she just stepped in, wrapped me up in a hug. For a moment, it was like everything else disappeared. The walls. The weight. The constant gnawing in my chest. All of it faded, and it was just me and her. And the quiet reminder that I wasn't alone.

When she pulled back, her hands stayed on my arms for a second, steady. *"You don't have to carry it all alone,"* she said, like she knew what I was thinking.

I exhaled, a shaky breath I hadn't realized I was holding. I nodded, but it was hard to find the words. *"I know. It just feels... like a lot."*

She gave me a look, her eyes soft, understanding. *"Yeah. It always does. But you've got me and Mom. And you've got Duke. And you don't have to carry it all on your own."*

I nodded again, the weight lifting just a little, like she'd pulled a corner of it off. It wasn't a fix, but it was something. A reminder. I glanced back toward Duke's room. The door was just ahead.

"Thanks," I whispered, barely enough to hear it myself.

Brittany gave me that smile again, the one that made everything a little easier to carry. *"Anytime."*

I turned back toward the door, taking a deep breath. Life wasn't easy—but we weren't meant to walk through it alone.

15 Whispers of Hope

Reality

I had the camera balanced on the porch railing, the late-April sun throwing lazy rays across the front yard when a warm breeze drifted by. It smelled weirdly sweet, like marshmallow chicks and Easter jelly beans, and it made me grin in that half-delirious way you do when the day just feels off-kilter. Ben was off to the side, slurping a soda and watching me film my so-called comedy sketches for YouTube.

"You know," I said, switching the camera on and flashing a dramatic sigh, *"I'm so stressed these days, I considered taking up yoga. Then I realized the only thing I can bend is my credit card."*

Ben nearly choked on his drink, his soft, loving brown eyes watering from laughter—the same eyes that reminded me I didn't have to lose myself. They helped me find my sense of humor, even through the pain. *"What the heck?"*

"Yeah, but it's true!" I threw my arms up in mock exasperation, adding a dramatic pause. With my crazy hazel eyes darting like I'd just had five cups of coffee, I said, *"My flexibility is at an all-time high. I can bend in exactly two ways: trying to touch my piggy toes and stretching my sense of humor to insane levels."* Then, with a dramatic flair, I bent down

and showed him, my fingertips barely grazing my toes. *"See? Impressive, right?"*

Ben howled, banging the porch railing, and for a moment, I felt the weight in my chest loosen up.

"You're the best, Ben," I expressed gently. *"You laugh with me, not at me. That means everything."*

It was like every laugh I got took a little piece of my fear and turned it into a joke instead. Whenever I remembered how close I came to losing him, my breath caught in my throat. Humor was the only thing that could crack open the panic, even if just for a second.

A few days later, we finally got the call that Duke was being discharged. The hospital's automatic doors whooshed behind us as Mom pushed his wheelchair forward, her hands tense on the handles. Duke, though, wasn't about to let a few bandages and weeks of bedrest kill his spirit—he wiggled his shoulders in a mock-dance, arms swaying like he was orchestrating an invisible band.

"Take me to the parking garage, please," he announced, half-singing each word.

Mom offered him a delicate smile as she steered him outside. I followed close behind, clutching the backpack full of meds. I know Mom felt joy that day too—a quiet kind of joy, tucked beneath the weight of everything we'd been through. And it was great to see her happy. She had endured so much.

The overhead fluorescent lights flickered, reflecting off Duke's gauze-wrapped arm. He whistled some tune, tapping his knees to a nonexistent drumbeat. For the first time in what felt like ages, the atmosphere wasn't suffocating; it was just a tired family heading home, sure, but heading home together.

In the dim light of the parking garage, Duke reached out, his fingers grazing the cold, rough concrete, as if he needed to confirm that this moment—this freedom—was real.

As the door clicked behind me, the crisp evening air nearly made me dizzy, washing away the sterile smell of the hospital. I paused on the stairs and turned to face the building that had changed so much for us, yet seemed utterly unaffected by it all.

Everything seemed lively and free outside in a way I hadn't seen in a long time, yet the silence within was heavy with sorrow. I took a shaky breath and let the cold air fill my lungs. I thought to myself, *God, you got me through this. Please continue to help me be strong.*

I could smell stale coffee and disinfectant on my jacket—scents that had practically become my everyday perfume—yet something about this moment felt brand new.

When we got him settled in the back seat, I let out this massive breath I didn't even realize I'd been holding. The scariest part was finally over. Sure, he still had a battle ahead—therapy, random pains—but watching him dance in that wheelchair? It felt like someone flipped on the *Hope* switch, and for once, I let myself believe things might actually be okay.

As I stood there, my gaze caught on words across a man's sweatshirt that reminded me of another glimpse in time I knew God was with me. The letters seemed to almost glow under the flickering parking garage lights, like the golden glow I remembered a few years back.

My mind wandered back to those California days when angels kept showing up in the most unexpected ways, reminding me to hold on, to trust, and to have faith—even when life felt like a tangled mess of unanswered prayers and endless questions.

The man strolled by us, slow and deliberate, and as he passed, he shot me a wink. Not just any wink—it felt like one of *those* winks, the kind that's not just a gesture but a nudge, a little heavenly reminder, almost like he knew exactly where my mind had gone.

It hit me then: God's presence—had continued to show up in my life, in the most beautiful and memorable ways.

Memories of the past swirled in my mind like leaves caught in a breeze, carrying me back to a time when faith was all I had to hold onto and angels seemed to walk the earth.

16 Golden Faith

Flashback

I wasn't over Billy—let's be real, not even close—but I kept myself busy, anything to dodge the emotional chaos. Somehow, after a modeling audition, I ended up in Scientology. Leaving it felt like escaping a maze I didn't even know I'd walked into. But hey, I was confident I'd made the right call to leave and ready to see what bizarre plot twist life had in store for me next.

I dove into background acting—TV shows, movies, commercials in Los Angeles, CA—you name it. Beach volleyball at Santa Monica Pier became my weekend ritual, spiking balls with my new crew under the sun.

Most days, I rode my red scooter through the hills of Los Angeles, bleach-blonde hair whipping in the wind beneath my red helmet. Speeding around forty miles per hour, it was just me, my tunes blasting on Pandora, God whispering in my ear, and a strange sense of peace that made me feel like I'd stumbled into a golden sunrise, even during my darkest hours.

The roads twisted and sparkled under the sunlight, mansions perched on the hills like castle fortresses, far away from Hollywood's madness. Some of those houses were my dream digs. The hills were brown, dotted with splashes of green plants, and the sky was usually a perfect blue with not a cloud in sight. Sometimes, the beauty hit me so hard I had to pull over, scoot to the side, and just watch it all.

Thoughts of how amazing life could be filled my mind—until reality hit me, which always seemed to happen at the gas station.

God would continually find me, just as He had always done, even when I didn't realize it. Standing at that gas pump, I was weighed down by the world, my thoughts a tangled mess of overdue bills, unanswered prayers, and the gnawing questions: *Where are You, God? Why can't I feel You near?* Yet He was there, as He always had been, patiently waiting for me to recognize His presence.

Like a thief that wouldn't leave, my worries clung to me. The rhythmic click of the pump and the climbing numbers felt like the relentless soundtrack to my never-ending anxiety.

Just keep going, I thought.

And then, there he was—a man I'd never seen before, stepping out of nowhere with a presence that felt... divine. Clean-cut, warm, and with a smile that reached deep into my guarded heart, he held out a gray sweatshirt. *Faith* was boldly embroidered across it in black and gold, catching the dim light like a beacon.

"You look cold," he said, his voice calm, steady, and knowing, as though he could see right through me.

For a moment, I froze, caught between disbelief and wonder.

"Oh, my goodness," I finally managed, clutching the sweatshirt like it was a gift too precious for words. *"Thank you. This is really... wow."*

He nodded, his kindness so casual it almost disguised the miracle of that moment.

"Pay it forward," he said before walking away, disappearing into the hum of the gas station like he'd never been there.

As I slipped on the sweatshirt, its soft fabric wrapped around me like a divine hug. The wind tangled my blonde ponytail, but I didn't feel the chill anymore. I glanced down at the bold letters stretched across my chest—*Faith*. A small smile crept onto my face, unbidden but welcome.

Los Angeles—the city where angels apparently show up with free merch.

How awesome, I thought, a mix of wonder and gratitude bubbling up inside me.

But this wasn't just about the sweatshirt. Not really. It was about the message, one that was written across my chest but felt like it was etched into my heart. God had been there all along—through every struggle, every doubt, every moment I thought He'd forgotten me. He hadn't.

He reminded me in the most surprising way that *faith will keep you warm*—through a stranger who appeared at the perfect moment. My soul echoed the epiphany: *Your faith will sustain you. Faith will never leave.* Even when I had been searching for Him, stumbling through life, He was there. God would continually find me, even in the ordinary moments, because His love never stopped reaching for me.

I rolled up the hills on my scooter, headphones blasting my favorite jams. Every wheel turn felt like a step further away from past negativity. But sometimes, when the shadows of my thoughts crept in, I just wanted to curl up and cry or scream. Even so, riding that red scooter felt like riding a magic carpet, a mystical escape where a hidden strength within me pushed me forward with a quiet, persistent *"Go"* when I wanted to stop.

One Saturday morning in late August, I decided to swing by Maria's nutrition store. Maria—my new California friend, who I'd met just a few weeks earlier—was the kind of person who made you feel like you could spill your heart while sipping a protein shake. My faith was on shaky ground, and my heart felt like it was lugging around a suitcase full of unanswered questions—again.

I parked my scooter in my usual spot (which, let's be honest, was just the closest spot to the door), kicked down the stand, and skipped toward Maria's. The door swung open harder than I'd intended, and before I knew it, I was sliding into my usual seat across from her desk—like a regular at a café, except my go-to order was advice, not coffee.

"Hi, Maria!" I said, forcing a smile as I tugged at my bleach-blonde ponytail—a nervous habit I couldn't seem to shake, especially when I knew someone could see my pain.

"Hey there, sweetie," she beamed, her rosy-red lips lighting up the room. There was something about her—an older, wiser energy—that made you feel like she already knew what you were about to say, but she'd let you say it anyway.

I glanced around the room, my eyes drifting over the shelves stacked with vitamins and powders that promised miracles in jars, before landing back on Maria.

With my tan hands rubbing my eyes, trying to catch a tear of confusion before it fell, I blurted out, *"Maria, I'm so confused. I'm a born-again Christian, and I prayed for God to lead me into healing, and somehow, I ended up in Scientology. Like, how does that even happen? My roommate said it's totally against the teachings of Jesus, and, honestly, she's probably right. But I've got to admit—those sessions made me feel lighter. For, like, five whole minutes. And then? Bam—all my burdens were right back, like they'd been on a coffee break and decided to clock back in."*

There they were again—those eyes, the ones that could see right through me. Maria, ever patient, chimed in as she filled a protein shake order. *"That's false hope, sweetie. It won't last. Only the healing from Jesus will. Keep praying to Him—He'll guide you, honey."*

Maria leaned in, her expression soft and understanding. *"Christy, I used to be Muslim before I saw Jesus. He appeared to me three times. He is love. Ask Him to reveal Himself to you, and He may appear. Ask Him to take control of your life, and He will show you the way. Jesus is full of love and forgiveness."*

I gasped, the words sinking in. *"Really? Wow!"*

"Yes. And if you feel anger toward anyone—even Billy—ask God to help you forgive them."

Time seemed to slow down. Our conversation about Jesus filled me with peace I hadn't felt in a long time.

"Can you tell me more about what you think about Scientology?" I asked, shifting in my seat. *"I don't go anymore after learning what they believe, but I heard about detoxing there, and it sounded interesting."*

Maria's eyes narrowed slightly. *"The best way to detox is with these affordable products I have here. They also help with hypoglycemia. I've known people in Scientology. Before you realize it, you're paying tons of money to find freedom—when you can have real freedom through Jesus."*

I grabbed my wallet, pulling out some cash I'd saved from working on the *Project X* set at Warner Brothers. *"Okay, what products are best for detox?"*

"I've got alfalfa, which is great, coconut oil, and..." She went into the details, explaining each product like she was selling sunshine. *"I'll get you set up."*

I handed her the cash, and she handed me my change with a warm smile. *"Enjoy, sweetie,"* she said, her voice deep but filled with love, wrapping around me like a comforting hug. *"And don't forget to talk to Jesus. He's always there, ready to listen."*

The bell jingled as another customer walked in, and I turned back to Maria, practically bouncing on my toes.

"Seriously, thank you," I said, my voice brighter than it had been in weeks. *"You're a lifesaver—well, technically, Jesus is, but you know what I mean."*

At the door, the customer held it open for me, her smile so fresh and calm it could've been bottled and sold as *"Hope"* in a Jar.

"Thanks!" I chirped, stepping past her and into the sunshine. My feet practically floated off the ground.

I didn't have it all figured out—not even close—but something inside me felt lighter, like I'd just stumbled on a secret too good to keep. Maybe I hadn't cracked the code yet, but I'd found another clue—one that brought me closer to understanding who Jesus really was and continued to be.

17 Sent from Heaven

Reality

Later that week, my mom, Brittany, Ben, and I took Duke to physical therapy, and they had him stand for the first time since before the accident. It was a milestone—one of those moments that takes your breath away because it feels like hope is finally winning. Joyful tears filled our eyes.

I heard my heartbeat as I stood there, eyes wide. He was unsteady, his legs shaking like a baby lamb's.

My heart melted when I saw the light of humility shine through him. As he stabilized himself on the parallel bars, his legs trembling from the effort, his remarks helped ease the tension. Duke, being Duke, was able to add some humor to the situation despite our fears that he would fall. He looked down at his shirt, a warm blue that was silky and inviting, like a fresh start.

"Blue's the color of new beginnings," he smiled, his voice light despite the strain in his body. *"Figured I'd dress for a picnic instead of a tornado."*

Everyone chuckled, the sound easing the tight knot of worry in the room. Leave it to Duke to turn a grueling moment into something almost poetic; after all, he was the rapper of the family. Even the therapist cracked a smile as they adjusted his posture.

"Well, if I fall, at least I'll do it with style." I felt terrified, but Duke seemed to be fearless.

"Duke, be careful, hon," Mom said softly, her voice filled with both worry and love. Her blonde hair shone in the light, framing her face like she was Duke's angel, always watching over him.

"Oh Lord Jesus, be careful," I blurted, my cheeks puffed up in sheer worry as I instinctively reached out toward him.

Duke turned his neck slowly to look at me, his expression was equal parts amusement and exasperation. Then he burst into a loud blast of laughter that echoed through the room, cutting the tension like a warm embrace.

I smiled and my cheeks deflated.

His hands flew up in dramatic flair, shaking just enough to make the gesture both humorous and heart-stopping.

"Ladies and gentlemen," Duke declared, his voice laced with exaggerated bravado, *"Watch and learn. I'm not falling. Not today."*

That was Duke. Though he was shaky, regaining strength, he was determined to fight through every ounce of pain. And seeing him fight like that, knowing how much it hurt, made every excuse I'd been clinging to feel small and ridiculous.

I stayed close, my hands hovering near his back like I could somehow catch him if his knees buckled.

"You're doing amazing, Duke," I said, though my voice wavered a little. *"Just don't get too wild, okay?"*

He grinned at me, sweat dripping down his temples. *"What's the fun in that?"*

He stood there for what felt like an eternity—seconds stretched into something holy, something I'll never forget. Then he finally lowered himself back into the chair.

Watching him stand, even for just a few shaky seconds, cracked something wide open inside me—the ability to learn how to begin to trust God through it all.

In that moment, watching Duke's defiant grin and trembling legs, I knew one thing for sure: he wasn't just surviving—he was fighting. Then I saw it—a sparkle of light in the corner of the therapy room. No one else noticed, but I did. *Was the angel there? The same one from long ago? Still with me, with us?*

The thought clung to me, filling my chest with something I couldn't quite name. Suddenly, my mind wandered back to that sparkling moment—the one that changed everything.

Flashback

That night, I went home with Maria's words lingering in my heart. *"Talk to Jesus. Ask Him to reveal Himself to you, and He may appear."* Her confidence inspired me. I wanted to see Him—not because I doubted, but because I longed to feel His embrace and to experience Him firsthand.

So, lying in bed, I whispered a quiet prayer: *"Jesus, I know You're there. If it's Your will, let me see You."*

The next morning, He answered my prayer.

I woke to the sound of my name. *"Christy, Christy, Christy."*

The voice was soft, melodic, and somehow familiar. It felt like it reached right into my chest, wrapping around my heart with the warmth of a home I had never felt before. At first, I thought I was dreaming, but the sensation was too real to ignore.

Then I heard it—the sound of something wrestling right in front of me. My heart raced as I tried to make sense of it. The room wasn't dark like it should have been. Instead, it was filled with light—not from the sun, though dawn was barely creeping in. This light was golden and alive, like it had its own pulse. It sparkled into every corner, chasing away the shadows.

For a split second, I thought it might be my California roommate, Jenna. I glanced over, but there she was, sound asleep, completely oblivious. That's when I turned back—and saw it. The most glorious, beautiful angel standing right beside my bed.

The light felt alive and encircled me in a peaceful, cozy hug rather than merely lighting the space. It seemed to be telling me in its head that everything would be alright as it stood there grinning with the happiest smile.

For a moment, time itself seemed to stop. Its blue eyes shone with so much kindness and understanding, it made my heart flutter in the best way. A soft glow surrounded it, radiating warmth that wasn't just felt—it sank deep into my soul. There was no fear, no doubt. I knew, in that moment, I could trust God completely.

I couldn't look away. Although, as I remembered I was on Earth and what I was seeing was not an everyday occurrence, my own human doubts started to creep in. As I began to blink, the glorious angel finally began to fade, the golden light dimmed, and the room grew quiet again. But the peace? The peace lingered, as if the angel had left a piece of itself behind—a reminder that God was always near, even when I couldn't see Him.

I sat there in the stillness, overwhelmed and humbled. He hadn't just heard me—He had answered. He sent me an angelic messenger, one I would never forget. With proof that I'd never walk alone.

18 The Comeback Game

Reality

A few months later, Duke was getting stronger. He asked me to play 1-on-1 basketball at Mom's, and, well, how could I say no? The cool night air brushed against my face as we stepped onto the cement driveway, the moonlight casting faint shadows across the familiar space. The driveway felt like it had its own memory bank, storing up all the games, laughs, and scraped knees over the years. Just standing there took me back to that night Duke taught me how to do layups before high school basketball tryouts.

Although, this time, was about life instead of just basketball. This time, hope and faith had laced up their sneakers and were with us on the court. Love was there too, in our midst. *Faith, Hope, and Love.* In that moment, they felt unshakable.

Across from me, Duke stood with a grin plastered on his face, looking like he'd just survived boot camp. Honestly, he deserved to smile like that.

He moved like he hadn't missed a beat, throwing every doctor's *"you'll never play basketball again"* prediction straight into the trash.

His gaze was fixed on the hoop as he dribbled the ball.

With that youthful Duke confidence that was equal parts adorable and infuriating, he teased, *"You're going down."*

I couldn't help but laugh, though there was something bittersweet about it.

"We'll see about that," I said, shaking my head as I tried to focus.

Not that I had much hope of winning—he was moving like he'd been training in secret. Every step, every dribble looked effortless, like he hadn't just been through hell to get there.

As I dribbled the basketball, my thoughts drifted. I had flashbacks to the past few years and realized how far we had come. Duke moved in the direction of the hoop as quickly as I was running out of breath. I attempted to keep up with him, but he blew by me like I was a turtle, and I gasped for air. Then, just to add salt to the wound, he finished with a layup so smooth I almost applauded. Almost.

"Damn, Duke, you smoked me!" I said, hands on my knees, trying to catch my breath while sweat poured down my face.

He laughed—a loud, carefree laugh that echoed through the night. The kind of laugh that makes you forget about the score, about everything else.

"Told you I'd win!" he said, grinning like a kid who'd just found the last piece of candy.

We both cracked up, our laughter bouncing off the driveway as we high-fived, my hand still shaky from exhaustion. And in that moment, none of it mattered—not the game, not the score, not even the past. What mattered was that we were there, under the stars, with *Faith, Hope, and Love* running the court right alongside us.

19 Rising Through the Ashes

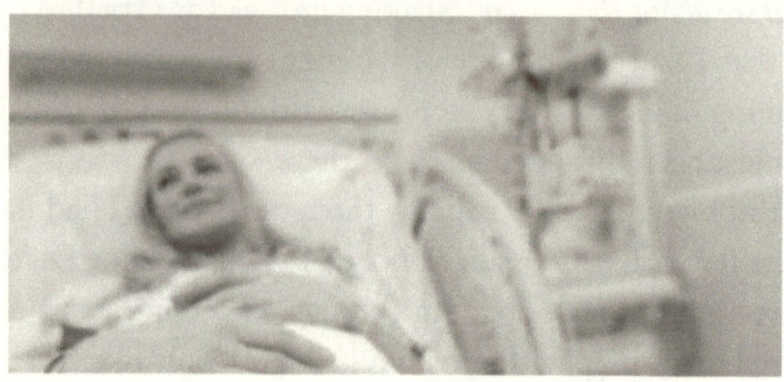

Flashback

I was back in my own memory battlefield—the sound of clanging weights and the constant hum of resolve filled the gym. I took hold of the kettlebell, feeling its icy metal against my palms, and raised it repeatedly, each movement a silent protest against the weight of my worries.

"You're letting it out," Marco said, his voice calm but encouraging. *"Every drop of sweat is another step forward."*

I managed a wry smile. *"Even the mess I keep dragging with me?"*

"Especially that," he replied with a knowing nod.

I let the kettlebell drop, its thud echoing through the room. For a moment, it felt like I had dropped more than just the weight.

Afterward, I stepped into the sauna, hoping to sweat away the tension still gripping me. I'd tried following what Scientology claimed would detox my body—not because I followed Scientology, but because I was desperate to lose weight and make my ex-boyfriend miss me. At first, the heat felt comforting, like a warm, protective blanket. But the moment I stood up, the world tilted.

Dizziness hit me hard, and I gripped the wooden bench to steady myself. *"Is it just me, or is the room spinning?"* I muttered, my heart racing.

Somehow, I made it to the bathroom. When I looked in the mirror, the reflection staring back at me didn't feel like mine. Pale skin, dark circles, a weariness that ran deeper than I was ready to admit.

"You've got to keep going," I whispered, gripping the sink as if it could hold me together. *"Please God, help me to live through whatever this is."*

The cold shower struck like a thousand pinpricks, each drop a jolt back to reality, a stark reminder of the limits my body refused to ignore. Dressing afterward was a slow, deliberate effort, my trembling hands fumbling with buttons and zippers.

At the snack bar, I tried to open a candy bar, but my hands shook too much. Frustrated, I leaned against the counter and asked the attendant for help.

"I think my blood sugar's low," I said, my voice weak.

The next thing I knew, paramedics were there, their movements quick and efficient.

"Her heart's going in and out," one paramedic said, leaning over me with his equipment.

I turned my head away from the chaos beside me—chaos meant to save my life—and remembered the angel I'd seen a few days prior. A wave of overwhelming peace washed over me, even as the scene around me blurred.

Just like my dad, whose thoughts were consumed by family when he was shot, I couldn't help but think of everyone—especially my sister. My family was 3,000 miles away, and I'd never felt so far from home. The paramedic's voices began to fade, blending into the background like a distant hum.

Then, sharp and urgent, another voice cut through the haze. *"We need to move now,"* one of them said, snapping me halfway back to reality.

My mind strayed to my parents—their fortitude and resilience in the face of so much grief and trauma—as the ambulance raced through the city, its sirens blaring. If they could overcome their struggles, perhaps I could too—we share the same blood, after all.

That day, the hospital room felt like a world of its own, sealed off from everything except the steady hum of machines. The pale blue walls closed in softly, while a faint, sterile smell lingered in the air. It wasn't exactly warm, but it wasn't entirely unkind either.

'God, where are You now? Where's the angel? Can't You show up just this once? I'm starting to feel scared. Am I going to be okay?'

My thoughts hung in the air like unanswered questions. But nothing did. Well, nothing except an oddly shaped bug on the ceiling. It didn't move, didn't scurry—just stayed there, watching me, or so it felt. And for some reason, in that moment, I'd never felt so much kinship with an insect in my entire life.

I continued to stare at the bug, just connecting with it in some crazy way.

The door creaked open, and in walked an older Asian doctor, clipboard in hand, face completely blank. No smile, no "how are you doing," just straight to business.

"Do you know what day it is?" he asked, glancing at me like he was sizing me up.

I blinked, torn between answering him and still feeling weirdly attached to my bug friend. *"Tuesday?"* I guessed, though I wasn't truly sure since I didn't work a Monday-to-Friday job.

"Good," he said, writing something on his clipboard. *"Do you know where you are?"*

"A hospital," I said, waving a hand toward the IV in my arm. *"I mean, I hope it's a hospital."*

He didn't react, didn't laugh—nothing. Just kept scribbling. *"You were severely dehydrated, and your potassium was dangerously low. California has free healthcare, so you're covered."*

"Oh, cool," I said, not really sure what else to say. *"Thanks, I guess?"*

Without a word, he pulled out two pills—gigantic, terrifying pills that looked like they belonged to a horse, not a human—and handed them to me along with a cup of water.

"These," he said. "And IV fluids."

I took the pills, trying not to gag as I swallowed them. Before I could even say thanks, he turned and walked out the door. *"Feel better,"* he said flatly, already gone before I could respond.

I stared at the door for a second, then looked back up at the bug.

The door creaked open again.

This time, I glanced up to see my roommate Jenna stepping in. Her blonde hair—pure, golden, and impossibly perfect, just like her figure—was pulled back in a loose braid, framing her face like she'd walked straight out of a magazine. She had that model-like elegance, the kind of beauty that made me do a double-take the first time we met.

For a moment, I had even mistaken her for the angel. And honestly, as she walked toward me now, moving with that same unshakable calm, I could almost believe it was there again.

She didn't need many words. Her hand found mine, warm and steady, and in that simple act, the tangle of fear and sudden grief inside me loosened, thread by fragile thread.

"I'm here, Christy," she said softly, her voice steady and sure.

It wasn't just words. It was a promise.

"It's time to go home," I murmured, the words carrying more weight than I expected. I wasn't sure what I meant by "home," but it felt right. Like letting go of something I'd been holding onto too tightly.

I experienced moments of joy along the way—glimpses of freedom that felt like the new beginning I needed, celebrated lessons that stretched my faith, and had encounters with genuinely intriguing people. God, however, seemed to be calling me back home.

California had run its course. I was broke, worn out from life's curveballs, and ready to go home.

20 Clouds Over Paradise

Flashback

Mom, Britt, and I were sitting on the balcony in Punta Cana, enjoying our vacation as the ocean breeze swirled around us. The warm air softened the distant sounds of Daniel's wedding, which drifted through the night.

Back at the hotel, the weight of the moment settled over me like a heavy blanket. Absentmindedly, I traced the rim of my glass, the quiet, rhythmic motion matching the loop of thoughts swirling in my mind.

"Where's Dad, Mom?" I asked, trying to sound calm, even though worry was clawing at me from the inside.

"I don't know, honey. Probably just down by the beach enjoying his evening," she said, her tone casual, like it was no big deal. But her answer didn't stop the knot in my stomach from twisting tighter.

Brittany was stretched out on the other hotel bed, her teenage eyes wide and innocent. I forced a small smile in her direction, trying to keep the worry from showing. She didn't need to carry this weight.

"He's been sober for 14 years, Mom. You don't think he'd drink, do you?" The words came out hesitant, my worry spilling over.

"Fourteen years," I repeated, as much to remind myself as her. My voice sounded steady, but inside, I was trying to convince myself it was true. *"He's worked so hard."*

I stayed sprawled on the hotel bed, staring at the ceiling while Mom walked briskly around the room, her pink shirt glowing against her beautifully tanned skin. She wasn't just moving—she was getting her steps in for the day, like this moment wasn't already heavy enough. It felt like the calm before a storm, and I wasn't sure if I was ready for what was coming.

Just then, the door swung open, and Dad stepped in. At first, nothing seemed off, but then I noticed it—the uneven shuffle in his steps, the way his glassy blue eyes stared out like he wasn't really all there. His brown hair was tousled, and something about him felt... wrong, like I was looking at a version of him from a time I didn't want to remember. My stomach twisted.

"No, no, no," Mom said sharply, rushing over to him.

My mind, uninvited, flashed back to when I was 12 years old, stirring up memories I didn't ask for. Still, I forced myself to stay present, rooted in the moment.

I froze, my chest tightening as waves of grief crashed within me. My thoughts tormented me with loud screaming questions I didn't want to answer. It felt like a tornado had stormed over my soul all over again.

'How could this happen? Why now? How could he let this slip after everything he's fought for?' Anger roared inside me, mixing with the panic, threatening to spill over like a storm I couldn't stop.

"Dad?" I said, my voice trembling, barely above a whisper. He didn't respond.

Mom rushed to his side, her hands reaching out to steady him. *"What happened? What did you drink?"* she asked, her voice trembling with desperation.

"I don't know," he mumbled, his words slow and slurred. *"I thought it was just... sparkling water."*

Mom turned to me, her face a mixture of panic and heartbreak.

"Someone must have given him the wrong drink," she said, her voice breaking, as if saying it out loud would somehow make it less true.

My heart pounded so hard it felt like it might burst. Anger clawed at my insides—I wanted to scream, to demand answers from him, from whoever handed him that drink, from the universe. But instead, I stood there, frozen, bitter, while the sick realization washed over me: this trip, this beautiful wedding, was about to turn into a nightmare.

Later that night, Mom, Britt, and I slipped out to the balcony. The warm, humid air felt stifling, like it was pressing down on my chest. Even the tropical breeze couldn't lift the crushing weight of what had happened. We joined hands and prayed, whispering our words into the darkness, hoping they'd somehow break through the storm around us. But deep down, doubt gnawed at me.

'What if this is it? What if this is the moment that breaks him? What if it breaks all of us?'

Dad tried—*God, he tried.* But there were days when his anger bubbled over, and staying sober felt like a mountain he just couldn't climb. The physical pain from his gunshot wound was constant, eating away at him, and for a moment, alcohol seemed to take the edge off. But it didn't fix anything—it only made everything worse.

21 Answered Prayers & Love

Reality

Addiction—it was a curse, and I hated every single thing about it. It crushed Mom and Dad, and fractured us all in ways we were still trying to piece back together. Mom carried so much more than anyone knew, but even her strength wasn't enough to hold it all. The strain drove a wedge between them, one that no amount of natural love could fix.

And yet, even after everything, hope and faith still lingered. It wasn't loud or flashy—it was more like that one plant that refuses to die no matter how bad you are at taking care of it. Quiet and persistent.

I heard it in her voice the day she called me.

"Hi, Chris," she said, her tone lighter than I'd heard in years.

"Hey, Mom," I said, sitting up straighter. *"What's going on? You sound... different."*

I was sitting on my red couch, legs tucked under me, scrolling aimlessly on my phone when Mom called. Her voice had this tone—steady but with a quiet excitement that made me sit up straighter. My heart skipped a beat before she even said anything.

"I have good news," she said, her words practically buzzing through the line.

"What? Tell me!" I said, dropping my phone onto the cushion beside me.

"It's Duke," she said, and my stomach flipped. Oh no. What now?

Her voice stayed steady, but I could hear the hope breaking through. *"He's in Christian rehab. I know rehab doesn't sound like the best news, but, Chris—he's been saved. Duke decided to truly follow Jesus. He's born again."*

I froze. *"Wait, what? Born again? Like... really born again?"* My voice cracked, excitement and disbelief tumbling out.

"Yes, honey. A true Christian born again," she said, and I could hear it—relief, joy, the sound of prayers being answered.

"Finally, God answered after 10 years," I said, my voice trembling with emotion.

"God works in mysterious ways," she said softly, her voice full of conviction.

I pressed my hand to my chest, trying to steady the rush of emotions. *"Wow, Mom, we've prayed for this for ten years. I can't believe this is actually happening! I have to go see him!"*

"I know," she said softly, her voice catching. *"But it is. It's finally happening."*

I leaned back into the couch, staring up at the ceiling as tears welled in my eyes. It felt surreal, like a decade of whispered prayers had finally been heard. Duke—born again. It was almost too good to believe. But a wave of grace and love washed over me in that moment.

22 Glimmers of Grace

Reality

Sunlight streamed through the window, annoyingly cheerful, as if it didn't have a concept of how thick the air felt. My cell phone buzzed on the nightstand, and Mom's name flashed across the screen.

As I reached for the phone, my stomach twisted. That feeling of unease hadn't left—it had only grown louder, like a storm brewing just out of sight.

"Hello?" my voice quivered.

"Mom?" Silence from the other end stretched so long that I steeled myself to hear bad news.

"Sorry, I was finishing my nutrition bar," she finally said after a second, her voice casual—but not casual enough to mask what lay beneath. *"How are you, sweets?"*

"You scared me! I thought something was wrong." My laugh sounded strained, a sad attempt at normal.

"Aww, did you hear? Dad's in the hospital again," she said, soft but steady. Her tone was the calm before the wave, and I braced myself, feeling like I was about to be dragged under.

"What? No! What happened this time?" I asked, holding onto the counter to ground myself.

"He fell and hurt his neck bad. The doctors said he could've been paralyzed. Thankfully, he's not. He's at Johns Hopkins."

That name. *Johns Hopkins.* It was a place etched into my memories: antiseptic smells, machine beeps, endless waiting. Dad's health had always felt like a tightrope walk—congestive heart failure, the drinking, the falls. He always pulled through, but it felt like we were just buying time.

"Is he going to be okay?" My voice weak with the weight of it all. *"When will these hospital visits end?"*

"I know, it's crazy, right? But yes, Dad should be okay. He might need neck surgery, but for now, he's stable."

"Can I visit him?"

"Of course. I'm going tonight. When are you thinking of going?"

"Tomorrow after work," I said, already dreading the fluorescent lights and the antiseptic. *"Are you sure he'll be okay?"*

"Yes, he's hanging in there."

A sharp pain took hold of my chest as I hung up and gazed at my phone. Even though my dad's weakness wasn't new, it always weighed heavily.

I sat there for a while, clutching the phone like it might somehow give me answers I knew weren't coming. The weight of Dad being in the hospital felt suffocating, relentless, like it was pressing the air right out of me. The tight knot of treacherous anguish in my chest made me want to shout and do something, anything. Instead, though, my mind drifted as if it were trying desperately to get away from the pain and fear that were dragging me down.

Flashback

We were at our favorite restaurant, the one with the antique red comfy seats. The champagne glasses caught the soft lighting just right, sparkling like tiny stars and diamonds, making the whole place feel magical. Outside, the November air was sharp and chilly, with golden leaves clinging stubbornly to nearly bare branches. But inside, it was warm, cozy, and ours. This wasn't just any place—it was where we had our first date two years ago.

That night, Ben seemed unusually quiet, his adorable brown eyes drifting around the room before finally locking into mine. It was our two-year anniversary, and I had the feeling he would propose. But there was this unspoken tension in the air—I knew he was about to propose and he was nervous.

We were halfway through dinner when he reached across the table and took my hand. Just like that. His fingers were warm, steady, and my heart started racing like it already knew something my brain hadn't caught onto yet.

"Christy," he said softly, his voice steady but a little lower than usual.

"What is it?" I asked obnoxiously loud.

The clink of glasses and quiet hum of the restaurant faded into the background. Then he smiled—that smile. The one that made everything else blur.

"Christy, you are my everything. I want to spend the rest of my life with you."

Before I could even process what he'd just said, he stood up. Right there, in the soft glow of candlelight, he pulled a small velvet box from his pocket. My breath caught as he dropped to one knee beside the table.

A rush of emotions hit me all at once—like I wasn't sure I even knew how to let myself feel joy, but deep down, I knew I was happy. I could feel it bubbling up from somewhere so deep it almost scared me. Time seemed to slow, or maybe my brain just decided to shut off entirely.

"Christy," he said, *"Will you marry me?"*

His voice was shaky, but there was something in it, something deeper—something that felt like forever.

Tears blurred my vision. How could this man, who had seen every messy, broken piece of me, love me like this?

"Yes," I whispered, my voice excited, and then louder, *"Yes!"*

A couple at a nearby table smiled and clapped softly, but I barely noticed. All I saw was him, sliding the most beautiful diamond ring onto my finger.

His warm brown eyes locked onto mine, as if silently promising, *I will take care of you. I will never hurt you.* And I believed it—because his eyes didn't lie.

In that moment, my heart could see the glimmering light shining through the cracks of my life. ***And that was everything.***

23 A Heavenly Gaze

Reality

Golden and steady, the sunset poured into my living room as if it was unaware of the weight bearing down on me. I gripped my phone as if it comforted me in those unsettling, unpredictable moments. Dad's voice replayed itself over and over in my head, and his last words, *"I love you,"* adhered to me like glue.

"Chris, I have to go," Dad said hurriedly.

Not those words again, I thought.

I tried to hold onto the tiniest glimpses of grace, clutching them like rare gems slipping through my fingers, disappearing faster than I could catch them. I felt unsettled, though.

I kept trying to convince myself that tomorrow's visit to Johns Hopkins would bring answers—maybe even a glimmer of hope. Deep down, I knew. Something terrible was coming, and there was nothing I could do to stop it.

The next morning, the sunlight cut through the blinds, compassionate and bright. My phone buzzed on the nightstand, vibrating with an urgency that made my heart race. And somehow, I almost felt the presence of that same angel—the one that seemed to show up in the quiet corners of my life—like something was gently protecting my mind from completely falling apart.

Momma's name lit up the screen. I answered, my breath catching the moment I heard her voice.

"Chris," she said, trembling, raw. "*I need you to come to Levindale Rehabilitation. Right now. This exact time.*"

"*What happened?*" I asked, my voice trembling as dread twisted in my stomach. "*It's only 7 a.m. Something happened. Is it Dad? Did he...?*"

Her sobs cut through the line, jagged and unrelenting. My insides dropped, and the earth shook beneath me. She didn't have to say anything—I already knew.

When I got there, the room was silent, impossibly still—like time had pressed pause.

Mom was sitting by Dad's bedside, clutching his hand like she could somehow hold onto him and keep him there. Her eyes were locked on his face, searching his unseeing blue eyes, like she thought she might still find him somewhere.

"*Mom,*" I whispered, stepping into the room, hesitant.

She lifted her head slowly, her red-rimmed eyes meeting mine. Her face was pale, drawn, and etched with a grief that words couldn't touch.

"*He's gone,*" she said softly, her voice barely audible, like anything louder might break her completely.

Grief was weighing me down like a thousand pounds. Then I caught him in a state of perpetual bliss.

Dad lay there, perfectly still, but his eyes—they were a blue more vivid than I'd ever seen before. They weren't empty; they seemed to shine, fixed on the ceiling with an expression of awe. It was as if he had just seen something far beyond this world, something divine. *I couldn't shake the feeling that the same angel who had visited me so many times before had revealed itself to him in his final moments.*

The air felt charged with something holy, like heaven had reached through the veil to guide him home, leaving behind a trace of its brilliance in his gaze.

He was gone.

And yet, a piece of him still lingered—not in the room, exactly, but in the memories we clung to like lifelines. Running through the forest, his voice calling out, *"Come here! You've got to see this!"* and there it was, a crayfish so big it looked like something out of a storybook. Dialing up that silly number to play the chocolate song—the one we'd dance to in the kitchen, laughing so hard it hurt.

All of it—the tears, the pain, the beauty—hit me at once, like a sled crashing into me during a cold winter storm, slamming into my chest and stealing my breath.

And then there was the supernatural love—the kind that somehow survived all the upheaval and trauma. It wasn't flawless, but it was real, and it was theirs. Yes, he was gone physically, absent from this reality, but the love and memories remained, alive and enduring.

Mom stroked his hand, her touch slow, deliberate, like she was trying to memorize every line, every crease, every detail.

Tears streamed freely down her cheeks, but her voice stayed steady.

She cried, *"I love you,"* so gently that it nearly vanished into the room's motionless silence. Then she said, *"I've always loved you,"* louder, as if she needed him to hear it.

She sat there, holding his hand, her gaze fixed on his face. And in that moment, the room felt both empty and full. Her words hung in the air, raw and final, like a truth she had to release.

I stood there frozen, my throat tight and my chest aching in ways I couldn't put into words. I wasn't sure if I was crying or just numb, suspended in the rawness of it all. Finally, I moved closer, sitting beside her and placing a hand on her shoulder.

"He knew, Mom," I said, my voice trembling. *"He knew you loved him."*

She nodded slowly but said nothing, her focus still entirely on him.

I stared at Dad's face, trying to reconcile the man I had known—the stubborn, complicated, deeply flawed man—with the stillness in front of me. He had carried so much pain, so many regrets. And yet, in that moment, he looked peaceful.

Later, as Ben held me close, the tears finally came, spilling out of me like a flood. I pressed my face into his chest and whispered through the sobs, *"Pain isn't wasted. It reshapes us—into love, into purpose."*

I looked up toward the heavens, where light filtered through the cracks in the clouds, and whispered a quiet prayer.

"Thank you, God—for the pain, for the miracles, and for Your glory."

24 Glory Through Pain

Reality

The snow fell gently, blanketing the world in quiet serenity as my wipers cleared the delicate flakes from my windshield. A tear slid down my cheek, warm against the chill in the air, as my father's voice echoed in my mind: *"Chris, one of these days, you're going to get your break, and something great will happen for you."*

My chest tightened, and I gripped the steering wheel a little harder. *Could this be one of those moments?*

I glanced in the rearview mirror, wiping away the streaks of mascara under my eyes. Behind me, the flurries swirled like tiny messengers of grace, soft and glorious, like the angel who always seemed to show up when I needed hope.

I had just taken the leap—leaving my teaching job to follow my dream of running **Passionate Motivation Volleyball.** I didn't know how it would all work out, but I trusted that God was leading me, step by step, and I clung to that trust wholeheartedly.

The winding back roads to our new home were surrounded by tall trees, their branches heavy with snow, bending gracefully under its weight. The valley opened up before me, and as sunlight peeked through the clouds, it sparkled onto the river, making the icy surface glisten like a thousand tiny diamonds. I smiled softly, then slammed on the brakes as a squirrel darted into the road.

I watched it hesitate, darting back and forth, unsure of its path. I laughed under my breath, shaking my head.

"That was me," I sang, watching it finally gather its courage and cross with purpose. *"Just a small creature who tried to find its way. Unsure at first, but eventually, I got there."*

I released the brake and drove the last stretch to the house.

As I pulled into the driveway, Ben stood outside the front door, bundled in his blue coat and smiling, waving like he'd been waiting all day just for me. The snow glistened behind him, and the river in the distance shimmered under the fading light. In that moment, it hit me: *This was home.*

Dad's voice echoed in my mind again: *"Chris, if you can impact just one kid's life... just one... you've done one hell of a job."*

Tears welled up as I glanced at the snow-dusted garden and then back at Ben, who walked toward me, his smile filled with love and warmth.

He opened my car door and held out his arms. The cool air stung my skin as I stepped into the warmth of his embrace. His arms wrapped around me, steady and strong, as if holding all my broken pieces together.

As he held me, he tilted his head down just enough to whisper, *"I'm here. Always."*

Those words melted into me, filling me with a sense of heavenly peace. Snowflakes drifted gently around us, their icy touch brushing softly against my cheeks.

Every scar I carried had built an unshakeable faith within me and had taught me to believe in the beauty of miracles. Through all of the trials, God quietly taught me the most profound truths: *Faith, Hope, and Love.*

"Glory through pain," I whispered, the words rising from my soul like a melody. They hung in the cold air, soft and steady, almost as if

they carried the strength of a miracle, shimmering with an unspoken grace.

I stayed there a moment longer, letting myself sink into the safety of Ben's arms. The tiny miracles of snow danced around us, sparkling like a scene from a wintry wonderland.

A small smile broke through me, a flicker of hope refusing to fade.

I didn't have all the answers, not even close, but in that moment, I knew one thing for certain: *I wasn't alone.* God's strength had carried me that far, and I felt deep in my heart that He would carry me through whatever came next.

A holy stillness filled the air, as if heaven itself had paused to listen. I smiled, meeting his eyes, and with a steady voice that carried through my tears, I whispered once more, *"Glory through pain."*

Acknowledgements

First, I want to thank my mom and dad, the two toughest and most resilient people I've ever known. You both taught me, in your own ways, that I could accomplish anything—no dream too big, no challenge too daunting.

Mom, your long hours of work, even when the weight of the world was on your shoulders, never went unnoticed. You showed grace and tenacity in getting our family through the most trying moments, and I am reminded of that strength every single day. You've taught me what it means to be resilient and to keep my head held high during life's most terrible storms. You're the reason I continually strive to grow, to do better, to be better. You've instilled in me the value of hard work, the strength of honesty, and the essence of real integrity—and I wouldn't be the person I am today without you.

And Dad—how do I even begin? Without a doubt, you were the most fearless person I ever knew. You've faced gunshot wounds, electrocution, spinal meningitis, broken ribs, a traumatic car accident, internal bleeding, blood clots, and heart failure—and through it all, you faced it with unwavering faith. If life tried to throw the kitchen sink at you, you'd throw it right back. You showed me what it meant to get up—again and again—no matter how hard the falls were. Thank you for teaching me that being fearless isn't about the absence of fear; it's about refusing to let fear win.

To both of you—thank you for being my constant inspirations. Your strength, courage, and love have sparked something in me: a fire to inspire others the way you've inspired me.

***Ben**, my husband, thank you for showing me that love—real love—is fearless. You taught me that falling in love again isn't just possible; it's beautiful.*

Brittany, *my sister, thank you for being my personal ray of sunshine. Even on the stormiest days, you somehow manage to make me laugh until my stomach hurts.*

Duke, *my brother, you're living proof that miracles happen. Thank you for reminding me to believe, even when it feels impossible.*

Jeff, *my older brother, thank you for saying volleyball was just a hobby. Without that comment, I might never have turned it into the passion and sport that became such a big part of my life.*

To all of you—you're my people, my rock, and my reason to keep going. Thank you for shaping me into who I am today.

Afterword

Are you ready to make Jesus the Lord of your life? To let go of trying to do it all on your own and trust Him completely? It's not about being perfect; it's about being willing.

Jesus loves you right where you are and wants to walk with you every step of the way. If you're ready, let's pray together and take that first step toward a new life in Him.

The Salvation Prayer

Dear Jesus,

I come to You just as I am—broken, searching, and in need of Your grace. I realize that I've made mistakes and fallen short of the life You desire for me, and I'm so sorry for the sins I've committed. Today, I turn away from those things, and I ask for Your forgiveness. Wash me clean, Lord, and make me new.

I believe that You died on the cross for my sins and rose again to give me life—life full of hope, purpose, and eternal joy with You. Thank You for that incredible love, even when I didn't deserve it.

Jesus, I surrender my heart and my life to You. Fill me with Your Holy Spirit. Let Your presence guide me, comfort me, and change me from the inside out. Teach me to walk in Your ways and to trust You in every step I take. I want to know You more deeply, love You fully, and live the life You've called me to.

Thank You for loving me, forgiving me, and never giving up on me. From this moment forward, I am Yours.

In Jesus mighty name, Amen.

Words from the Author

Author: Christina Callahan
Photographer: Juliana Brito

I wrote because I had no idea what else to do. At the time, it felt like the only thing keeping me together—a desperate attempt to pour out every ounce of strangling emotions that were tying knots inside me. I wasn't even sure what I was looking for—clarity, peace, maybe a little more hope. Or maybe I was just trying to survive the storm in my head long enough to catch my breath.

Now, 14 years later, those raw, tear-soaked journal entries have turned into something I never could have expected. It started with me, alone with my thoughts—wrestling with God, questioning every storm that hit, and grasping for even the faintest flicker of light in all the chaos. By the Grace of God, all of that has grown into this book.

Sources:

The Holy Bible: New King James Version. Thomas Nelson, 1982.

About the Author

I've been happily married for 10 years, but let me tell you—I spent way too much time chasing love in all the wrong places until, thankfully, he found me. I'm a Christian who loves God deeply, but I don't believe in arguing about it. I'd much rather spread the gospel and good news with love and let people live their lives. To each his own, right?

I have a quirky sense of humor that sneaks into my writing because, let's face it, life's too short to be serious all the time. I'm a creative person at heart. I enjoy diving into everything that excites me, whether it's spiking a volleyball, starting a business, or writing down my ideas. I guess you might say that I just like creating stuff.

Being a motivational speaker and assisting others in overcoming obstacles and rediscovering hope is one of my greatest pleasures. Nothing is more satisfying than witnessing someone discover they are stronger than they once believed.

When I'm not juggling all of that, you'll probably find me daydreaming, finding humor in the silly things about life, or spending time with my amazing husband—the one who found me after I stopped searching in all the wrong places. Writing is my way of opening my heart, sharing my faith, and hopefully making you laugh, think, or feel a little less alone. Let's take this journey together!

Read more at https://christycallahanspeaks.com/.